Helen Corbitt's
GREENHOUSE
COOKBOOK

Also by Helen Corbitt

HELEN CORBITT'S COOKBOOK

HELEN CORBITT'S POTLUCK

HELEN CORBITT COOKS FOR LOOKS

HELEN CORBITT COOKS FOR COMPANY

Helen Corbitt's

GREENHOUSE
COOKBOOK

HELEN CORBITT

Illustrations by Jean Meyer

HOUGHTON MIFFLIN COMPANY BOSTON

Library of Congress Cataloging in Publication Data
Corbitt, Helen.
Helen Corbitt's Greenhouse cookbook.
Includes index.
1. Cookery. 2. Greenhouse, Arlington, Tex.
(Resort) I. Greenhouse, Arlington, Tex. (Resort)
II. Title. III. Title: Greenhouse cookbook.
TX715.C799 1979   641.5   79-11149
ISBN 0-395-25729-8

Printed in the United States of America

M 12 11 10 9 8 7 6 5 4 3

Acknowledgments

THE TEDIOUS WORK connected with calorie counting and the conversion of U.S. standard measurements to metric equivalents was done by Frances Holloran, R.D., a former co-worker and long-time friend. Her enthusiasm for each menu and recipe made the workdays short as we reminisced about our days at New York Hospital, where we once held forth in the private pavilion.

I also wish to thank Bertha Shields and Barbara Britt, supervisors of The Greenhouse kitchen, for their generous willingness to welcome changes in menus and service.

Resources used for calorie computations were *Food Values of Portions Commonly Used*, twelfth edition, by Bowes and Church, and *Nutritive Value of American Foods*, Agriculture Handbook No. 456, Agricultural Research Service, United States Department of Agriculture.

HELEN CORBITT

Contents

Acknowledgments vii

PART I

Introduction 3
Gentle Rules and Regulations 8
A Note on Metric Measurements 13

PART II / A MONTH OF MENUS

Breakfasts 17
First Week 20
Second Week 26
Third Week 31
Fourth Week 36
Sundays 41

PART III / RECIPES

Soups 47
Salads and Their Dressings 59

Cheese and Eggs   73
Vegetables   79
Seafood   90
Poultry   97
Meat   108
Low-Calorie Desserts   118

PART IV

Greenhouse Indulgences   135
A Potpourri   149
This and That   163

PART V

Glossary of Frequently Used Cooking Terms   177
Caloric Content of Common Food Items and Beverages   179
Index   187

PART I

Introduction
Gentle Rules and Regulations
A Note on Metric Measurements

Introduction

IN SEPTEMBER 1965, in an extravagantly beautiful setting in Arlington, Texas, the luxurious health and beauty spa known as The Greenhouse opened its doors. Owned by Great Southwest Corporation, with promotional assistance from Neiman-Marcus and Charles of the Ritz, it soon became one of the most famous spas in the world. I was invited to join the staff as Food Consultant and was involved in planning and preparations from the very beginning.

The Greenhouse was established as a haven of escape for women. Some guests seek escape from family and social pressures only, while others, professional women, need release from the rigid demands of business, medicine, teaching, the theater, television, and other careers. Women come not only from all over the United States but from many other places, particularly Canada, Mexico, and Europe. Through the years The Greenhouse has been a popular retreat for writers, artists, and philanthropists. And politicians' wives — as well as women politicians — have enjoyed the sanctuary of The Greenhouse and its health-giving, nerve-soothing program. The serene landscaping with its abundance of growing things does for the

[3]

guests what a greenhouse does for its plants: it nurtures them to good health. It is always a great satisfaction for The Greenhouse staff to see a guest leave with a new spring in her step, brighter eyes, clearer skin, and a look of genuine well-being.

As Food Consultant to The Greenhouse, I design the series of menus and recipes used in the program. The menus are based on the simple fact that from the standpoint of good health, foods that are low in calories, and especially foods that are low in saturated fats, are better for everyone, regardless of age or sex. Fresh fruits and vegetables, whole grain cereals and breads, and in fact all foods that are prepared properly to preserve their essential food value produce the elements necessary for good health. The Greenhouse selects only the best quality foods and, to preserve their vitamins, prepares them just minutes before serving.

I contend that regardless of what kind of food you eat, or how many calories it contains, you will enjoy it more if it is served with style and flair. My menus provide contrasts not only among the flavors and textures of the foods served but also — and this is most important — among the colors. Serving implements and accessories should complement each other as well as the food. To go with the Limoges, Aynsley, and Herend china presented on the breakfast trays in the guests' rooms each morning, I chose Irish linens in pastel colors. The linens I selected for the elegant formal dinners are appropriate background for the Royal Crown Derby and Limoges china, the Waterford crystal, and the sterling silver. Informal luncheon around the indoor pool is served on Italian pottery that carries out the garden theme of lunching among blooming flowers and plants.

I began my career as a therapeutic dietitian. My main object in planning food for The Greenhouse has been not to design a crash diet for a week or two, but to introduce The Greenhouse guests to a basic program for themselves, their families, and the friends they entertain. Some of them return every year to pick up the latest recipes and other new ideas that have been incorporated into The Greenhouse regime.

In planning menus I keep in mind the season, as we use only fresh fruits and vegetables at their prime. Meats are carefully selected from the finest available; fresh seafood is flown in from Boston, not frozen but iced. Except for breakfasts, there are no repeated menus in a three-week stay.

To encourage the guests' interest in preparing and serving low-calorie food, I sometimes conduct a mini cooking school. The guests come to The Greenhouse kitchen at 7:45 on a Saturday morning, and I show them how to cut, cook and serve the foods they have been eating that week. It always amazes me to see how many guests come again and again to this early morning gathering, but each session is different, as the menus change, and I discuss new dishes and techniques.

Everyone always wants to know how we slice the famous Greenhouse orange to look so tempting, how we make the Melba toast, and how we slice a 3-ounce tenderloin steak to look like a 10-ounce sliced sirloin. It is my only opportunity to talk individually with the guests, to destroy some food myths and old wives' tales, and to encourage better cooking and eating habits generally. I stress family health along with individual health.

All during their stays I see these guests in their yellow terry-cloth robes with no make-up, and they see me the same way. So it is most rewarding for me to have a former guest, beautifully coifed and dressed, approach me in an airport or hotel lobby to thank me for having taught her to slice oranges exactly as they are served at The Greenhouse — and to express her appreciation to me for my part in getting her husband and children to eat vegetables.

In the following chapters I give you the diet routine followed at The Greenhouse. You can follow it at home and you can include your family. The menus are balanced to contain all food groups: some fats and carbohydrates, foods with high protein content, and foods high in vitamins and minerals. For special occasions, and for people who don't need to watch their weight, I have also included in this book two chapters full of less dietetic treats: Greenhouse Indulgences and A Potpourri.

Please remember that diet alone very seldom takes off inches. Exercise in some form must go along with a good diet, as it does at The Greenhouse. And exercise not just once in a while, but every day. The exercise does not have to be strenuous and it can be your favorite: golf (without a cart), tennis, horseback riding, swimming, bicycling. And remember my favorite advice: a two-mile walk each day never hurt anyone.

The exercise program at The Greenhouse, famous for its results, was designed by and is under the supervision of Toni Beck, well-known choreographer and head of the dance department of Southern Methodist University in Dallas.

Guests are given a medical examination by Dr. James R. Almand, Jr., director of the medical department of The Greenhouse, before the diet and exercise schedule can begin. During a guest's stay, Dr. Almand, the nurses and I confer on each guest's progress and suggest modifications in her regimen to heighten its effectiveness. Any change in procedure is made with his permission and advice.

I suggest that before following The Greenhouse program of diet and exercise as presented in this book, you should first check with your family doctor. Tell him which exercise you have chosen to accompany your reduced caloric intake. Show him the menus and recipes. Then, with his permission, give The Greenhouse way a month's trial. At the end of that period you will be able to see the results and add the correct types of food for a maintenance diet. Increase sensibly, by adding from 3 to 6 ounces of lean meat, fish or poultry, more vegetables, and whole grain cereal and bread.

[6]

The menus in this book, based on 850 calories a day, can be a guide for you in your daily life at home. They are also a reliable guide to the kinds of foods you should emphasize in a program of maintenance eating that will keep you trim and healthy. Remember this when you are tempted to go back to the old habits. The Greenhouse way of eating, combined with regular exercise, can form the basis for a healthier life-style and many rewards. Not only will you feel better but, as your silhouette improves, your natural beauty will shine through.

I wish you a happy, active life.

Gentle Rules
and Regulations

AMERICANS — and others, I'm sure — use too many sauces, too much salt, and too much alcohol. Gastronomically speaking we have too much going down our intestinal tracts, too often.

Americans move too little to burn up the calories generated by the food we eat. If we all walked more instead of driving, using escalators, or taking cabs, if we carried our packages instead of having them delivered, if we lived in homes where we had to go up and down stairs, there would be fewer weight problems for those who enjoy eating.

Simply put, the vast majority of people who become overweight do so because they eat more calories than they expend in exercise. The following statements ought to be memorized by everyone:

> When caloric intake equals caloric output, weight remains unchanged.
> When caloric intake is greater than caloric output, weight goes up.
> When caloric intake is less than caloric output, weight goes down.

The chart below plainly spells out to you just how much energy you must expend to burn up the calories you take in. I chose walking as an example because this is what I do most.

Energy Equivalent Chart

Food Items	Calorie Content	Walking
BEVERAGES		
Beer, 8-ounce glass	114	22 minutes
Martini, 3½-ounce glass	140	27 minutes
Scotch, 1½-ounce jigger	105	20 minutes
Wine, 3½-ounce glass	84	16 minutes
Carbonated drinks, 8-ounce glass	106	20 minutes
Chocolate malted milk	502	97 minutes
Milk, 8-ounce glass	166	32 minutes
Milk, skim, 8-ounce glass	81	16 minutes
BREAKFAST FOODS		
Bacon, 2 strips	96	18 minutes
Pancake (1) with syrup	124	24 minutes
Doughnut	151	29 minutes
Egg, fried	110	21 minutes
Egg, boiled	77	15 minutes
LUNCH AND DINNER ENTRÉES		
Cottage cheese, 1 tablespoon	27	5 minutes
Cheddar cheese, 1 ounce	111	21 minutes
Turkey, 1 slice	130	25 minutes
Club sandwich	590	113 minutes
Steak, 3 ounces	235	45 minutes
Hamburger	350	67 minutes
Tuna fish salad	278	53 minutes
Potato chips, 1 ounce	108	21 minutes
Crabmeat, ½ cup	68	15 minutes
Fried shrimp, 6	180	22 minutes
Haddock, 1 piece, steamed	71	14 minutes

VEGETABLES, SALADS, ETC.

Potato, 1 medium, boiled	100	19 minutes
Raw carrot, 1 medium	42	8 minutes
Lettuce, 3 large pieces	30	4 minutes
Peas, ½ cup	56	11 minutes
Spinach, fresh, ½ cup	20	2 minutes
Mayonnaise, 1 tablespoon	92	18 minutes
French dressing, 1 tablespoon	59	11 minutes

DESSERTS AND FRUITS

2-layer cake, 1/12	356	68 minutes
Chocolate chip cookie, 1	51	10 minutes
Ice cream, 1 scoop	193	37 minutes
Apple pie, 1/6	377	73 minutes
Strawberry shortcake	400	77 minutes
Apple (large), 1	101	19 minutes
Banana (small), 1	88	17 minutes
Orange (medium), 1	68	13 minutes
Peach (medium), 1	46	9 minutes

Source: F. J. Konishi, "Food Energy Equivalents of Various Activities," *Journal of the American Dietetic Association*. Reprinted from *ADA Forecast*.

After a thoughtful reading of the Energy Equivalent Chart you may decide to eliminate the potato chips from a salad plate or as a snack. Choose cottage cheese instead of a hamburger, spinach over peas. And forget the pancake entirely.

Some Do's and Don'ts

1. When you get up in the morning, drink at least 1 glass of water. You'll be surprised how good it will taste. Drink more than 1 glass if possible. Then continue to sip water throughout the day, aiming for a total of 8 glasses.
2. Walk around the house or apartment while your morning

coffee is brewing, or go outside and walk briskly around in the yard.

3. Do not skip breakfast, and be sure to include fresh fruit. Vitamin C has a lot going for it.

4. Cut down or cut out sugar, and, remember, 1 tablespoon of honey has 64 calories.

5. Cut down on salt. Use a good vegetable salt instead. I like Vege-Sal, which contains some sodium chloride, sea salt, and finely ground vegetables and provides the flavor you think you need.

6. Use skim milk in place of whole milk.

7. Use unsaturated vegetable oils and margarine.

8. Solid butter and solid margarine contain the same number of calories. When they are whipped the count is much less. You can make your own whipped margarine by adding water or skim milk to solid margarine and whipping it at high speed in your blender or food processor.

9. If using canned fruits or seafood, choose varieties that are packed in water rather than in heavy syrup or in oil.

10. Sugar substitutes are still being tested for possible harmful effects. Please use them only in limited amounts. You may prefer to substitute sugar, honey, or some other sweetener for the sugarless sweetener suggested in my recipes. If so, you should know that my measurements are based on Sweet'N Low, which is ten times as sweet as sugar. A recipe calling for a teaspoon of sugarless sweetener would therefore require 10 teaspoons of sugar, or about 3 tablespoons, to come out right. Be sure to make similar adjustments if you are using a sugar substitute that is either sweeter or less sweet than Sweet'N Low.

11. Remember that seafood and chicken have fewer calories than red meats.

12. Broil, roast, or boil meats, fish, and chicken, using little or no added fat.

13. As much as possible, use fresh fruits and vegetables. You can always find them if you make an effort, perhaps not the specific item you had in mind but something fresh and good.

14. Do not overcook anything. Preserve those vitamins.
15. Do not use condiments like catsup or chili sauce unless you include their calories in the total for that dish.
16. Breads and cereals are better for you if made from whole grains. There is no appreciable difference in calorie count, but high fiber is necessary for good health.
17. Do not drink alcohol. Cut out or limit soft drinks.
18. If you must have soft drinks, choose varieties that don't contain sodium.
19. Buy a kitchen scale. In a few years every recipe will be in ounces and grams anyhow.
20. Liquors and wines may be used in cooking only. Do not take a sip of either while you are measuring the size of your portions for cooking.

A Note on
Metric Measurements

THE METRIC CONVERSION ACT, passed by Congress in 1975, provides for voluntary conversion to the metric system of measurement in ten years. This has been advanced five years and is fast becoming accepted, as you may note from weights and volumes on packaged products. But it is not going to come in a hurry, and for all practical purposes you can still use standard U.S. ingredient measurements. So do not panic over it, and do not throw away your old cookbooks.

I have written these recipes with both U.S. standard and metric measurements. The metric weights and volumes are given in parentheses following the U.S. measures. For your convenience in the kitchen I have rounded off the precise metric measures to the nearest reasonable unit: for example, .59 mL is given as ½ dL, 2366 mL as 2½ L, 232.2°C as 230°C, etc. I have not bothered to convert small measurements such as a teaspoon or fractions thereof, and a pinch is still a pinch.

Be sure to use standard measuring utensils. A teacup is not a measuring utensil, nor is a jigger, nor a handful. New measuring cups and containers are marked with both metric and U.S. units. Glass and clear hard plastic are more convenient than opaque materials.

PART II

A MONTH OF MENUS

THIS SECTION provides menus for four six-day weeks, followed by some special suggestions for Sundays. Each daily menu is designed to furnish approximately 850 calories, including a light breakfast which you may vary within the guidelines discussed below. Recipes are provided for all menu items that are capitalized.

Breakfasts

Let's get the whole month of breakfasts out of the way first. You may find that you resist change early in the morning, but you must pare down that heavy meal you may have been eating. So it's goodby to pancakes and French toast and pastries, but there are other more delicious things in store for you.

Eat breakfast. Every day!

Start with fresh fruit. For example, an orange, ½ grapefruit, whatever fruit is ripe, the equivalent of ½ cupful. Then have an egg or 1 ounce of low-fat cottage or farmers' cheese or 2 very thin slices of Canadian bacon or 2 slices of very crisp bacon. Also include, if you like, 1 thin slice of whole wheat or health bread toast (many people cannot tolerate coffee and fruit or an egg without bread of some kind). Gluten toast is quite delectable; customers at "21" in New York City get irate when the restaurant runs out. Or choose, in place of bread, ¾ cup whole grain cereal and ½ cup skim milk. You may have tea or coffee, decaffeinated if you prefer, black or with skim milk. Vary breakfasts as much as possible.

Don't get in a rut. Read on to see just how many lovely fresh fruits there are and what a choice you have.

Fruits

½ grapefruit, iced or baked, or its juice
1 medium orange, sliced, sectioned, or its juice
1 medium peach, fresh or steamed
1 medium Bartlett, Comice, or Bosc pear, fresh or steamed
1 small apple, fresh or steamed
¼ cantaloupe
⅛ honeydew, Spanish, or casaba melon
½ cup berries, any kind
½ small papaya
½ cup ripe mango
½ medium banana
1 tangerine
3 apricots, fresh or steamed
½ cup fresh pineapple
2 small fresh figs
10 grapes
3 small stewed prunes with 2 tablespoons juice, no added sugar
1 kiwi fruit (a delicious, funny-looking green fruit with brown fuzz all over it; just peel and slice it)

Few fruits need sweetening. Stay away from sugar. Use artificial sweeteners if you must, but try to get acquainted with the pure fruit flavor.

Eggs

You need protein to start the day with: 1 egg, soft-boiled, hard-cooked, poached in water or skim milk, or baked in a covered ramekin or cooker. Or scramble it without butter (prepare the pan with nonstick vegetable spray), but add 1 teaspoon cottage cheese and you'll enjoy it more. And an omelet with 1 added egg white, some herbs, or a few gratings of Parmesan cheese, will set you up for the day. Remember that the calories are concentrated in the yolk; a medium-size egg has 52 calories in the yolk, 15 in the white. If you are too worried about calories and cholesterol, skip the yolk. While the yolk has more calories than you may think you would like, it has, among other things, iron, copper, and Vitamin A, and you need them all.

First Week

Monday

It is not wise to skip lunch. You are usually hungrier for dinner if you do. If you live alone, and can eat your heavier meal at noon, so much the better for dieting results.

½ papaya filled with ½ cup cold cooked shrimp on bed of
  soft lettuce. I use tiny Greenland or Pacific Bay
  shrimp because they look better and taste sweeter than
  larger ones, but use whatever is available. Sprinkle with
  1 tablespoon of lime juice and a few gratings of coconut,
  about 1 teaspoon
3 stalks hot or chilled asparagus, fresh, frozen, or canned.
  If hot, sprinkle with 1 teaspoon of grated lemon peel,
  chopped pimiento, and parsley; if cold, serve on a bed of
  watercress or soft lettuce with 1 teaspoon Vinaigrette
  Dressing
black coffee or tea

Papayas are available most of the year in all parts of the country, but if your greengrocer has none, create the market for them by telling your friends how good they are. They will do the rest!

Of course you should take your coffee and tea without sugar or cream, but add skim milk if you must. In counting calories for milk in your coffee or tea, allow about ¼ cup, 25 calories. Most sugar substitutes are about 3 calories per serving.

Water-packed tuna fish, crabmeat, or chicken could be substituted for the shrimp; with chicken, add 1 tablespoon low-calorie yogurt mixed with ¼ teaspoon Dijon mustard. Keep this combination made up in your refrigerator for salads, vegetables, seafood — 1 cup low-calorie yogurt plus 1 tablespoon Dijon mustard and 1 teaspoon lemon juice.

If you have a letdown in the afternoon around 3:30 or 4:00, ½ cup cut-up fresh fruit in the blender or food processor with 1 cup of ice and fresh mint makes a delicious pick-me-up, as does ½ cup skim milk or ½ cup bouillon.

DINNER

Eat dinner at 7:00 P.M. or shortly thereafter. Kick the 9:00 or 10:00 habit.

Jellied Vegetable Consommé
Marinated Flank Steak
Stir-fried Spinach with 1 teaspoon grated carrot sprinkled
    on top
Turnip Pudding
¼ head romaine lettuce with 1 teaspoon Red Wine Vinegar
    Dressing
chilled steamed fresh peach or pear with 1 tablespoon of
    puréed strawberries or raspberries as a sauce
demitasse

Unless otherwise stated, 1 teaspoon of salad dressing is enough for a small salad and 1 tablespoon of a dessert sauce, such as custard or puréed fruit, is allowed.

Tuesday

LUNCH

A cooked vegetable lunch, served either hot or cold, should be a part of a diet regime. This is one of my favorites: as many kinds of steamed vegetables as you like, about ¼ cup each to make a total of 2 cups. Arrange them on a platter in rows and eat one row at a time. This way you always seem to have more left to eat. For instance, a row of julienned, fresh cooked beets; a row of slivered green beans; a row of julienned carrots; a row of sticks of zucchini; a row of blanched cherry tomatoes covered with sautéed mushrooms; a row of small, diced white turnips; a row of broccoli buds topped with spring onions.

Cold, marinate with Vinaigrette Dressing; hot, sprinkle lavishly with grated lemon or orange peel, chopped parsley, and sliced green onions. In a steamette the vegetables may all be cooked at one time. Serve with 4 ounces cottage cheese.

For dessert, have ½ cup grapefruit sections marinated in apricot nectar; and tea or coffee.

DINNER

spinach, mushroom, and orange salad with Vinaigrette
　Dressing
Coq au Vin
½ cup shredded Zucchini
Carrots in Vodka
½ Baked Custard with Orange Sauce
tea or coffee

Wednesday

LUNCH

salade minerale: Fill 5 lettuce cups respectively with ½ cup marinated grated carrots, ½ cup marinated grated radishes, ½ cup marinated grated zucchini squash, 1 small sliced tomato, and 2 ounces slivered Swiss cheese; put a bunch of watercress in the center.

tea or coffee

Use Vinaigrette Dressing for the marinade.

DINNER

cucumber boat filled with ¼ cup (3 medium) chopped shrimp mixed with 2 tablespoons chopped celery, 1 tablespoon mustard and horseradish sauce

Ginger Roasted Chicken

½ cup Stir-fried Vegetables (use bean sprouts, green peppers, and sliced onions)

½ cup steamed broccoli flavored with a few drops of anise

1 warm steamed peach with 2 tablespoons apricot nectar

demitasse

Thursday

LUNCH

2 ounces thinly sliced, cold, roasted lean meat

green chile and tomato salad with Niçoise Dressing

Pears Poached in Red Wine

tea or coffee

demitasse of Beet and Yogurt Soup
1 large knuckle of Osso Buco
1 small zucchini boat filled with ¼ cup Ratatouille,
   sprinkled with Parmesan cheese
¼ heart of romaine lettuce with ¼ cup shredded radishes,
   Vinaigrette Dressing
½ cup Orange Ice in orange shell
tea or coffee

Friday

LUNCH

Crabmeat Chantilly
spinach and grapefruit salad with Sherry French Dressing
tea or coffee

I like to use spinach in place of lettuce in salads; it has more
flavor and color, for the same calories. Use whatever pleases
your palate.

DINNER

Gratin of Celery
Trout with Red and Green Pepper Sauce
¼ cup baked potato skins
½ cup cooked fresh green beans and okra with grated
   lemon peel
Low-Calorie Cheesecake
demitasse

If at all possible, use fresh fish. It tastes better. If frozen, defrost it in skim milk, then dry it thoroughly.

Saturday

Shrimp and Spinach Quiche
1 average-size cooked or canned beet and raw endive salad
   with Vinaigrette Dressing
fresh fruit of your choice
tea or coffee

D I N N E R   W I T H   G U E S T S

Any variety you can introduce into your dinner routine makes you a happier person — and this applies to people as well as food. Even if you are not the kind of person who habitually invites friends for dinner, do it once in a while. Do not go off your diet; do not reveal that you are on a diet. Learn to keep a secret. I serve diet food to guests frequently and receive nothing but compliments and requests for the recipes.

hors d'oeuvres: cherry tomato filled with finely chopped
   water chestnuts or celery; marinated canned artichoke
   hearts; 1-inch squares of feta cheese; pickled shrimp
Tandoori Roast Chicken
½ cup sautéed mushrooms and onions
Watercress and Potato Salad
fresh fruit of your choice
demitasse

Limit yourself to one each of the hors d'oeuvres, or even less.

Second Week

Monday

LUNCH

Chicken Yakitori
Sliced artichoke bottom and spinach salad with 1 teaspoon
    Sesame Dressing
coffee or tea

DINNER

Minted Pea Soup
Veal Stew with Zucchini
½ cup steamed leaf spinach with Parmesan cheese
½ cup Celery Root Salad
½ cup lemony Soft Custard
demitasse

Tuesday

LUNCH

3 ounces sliced white meat of chicken
½ cup Vegetables à la Grecque
coffee or tea

DINNER

cold Carrot Soup with 1 teaspoon mashed avocado
Oriental Beef
½ cup fresh broccoli soufflé (see Artichoke Soufflé)
½ cup slivered Belgian endive salad with 1 tablespoon
   Sherry French Dressing
fresh pineapple boat (⅛) with 1 tablespoon puréed
  strawberries
demitasse

Keep some base for the carrot soup made up in your freezer.
When you need it, just add milk and heat it up; or serve it
cold.

Wednesday

LUNCH

1 cup Vegetable Chowder
Antipasto Salad
coffee or tea

DINNER

½ cup sliced fresh fruit with 1 tablespoon Cottage Cheese
    Dressing
Poached Turbot
½ cup steamed fresh green beans with dill
tomato, cucumber, and spinach salad with 1 tablespoon
    Buttermilk Dressing
Vanilla Ice Cream
demitasse

Thursday

LUNCH

Clam and Mushroom Soup
Crabmeat and Grapefruit Salad
½ cup Baked Custard
coffee or tea

DINNER

1 small peeled tomato filled with ¼ cup finely diced raw
    vegetables and ¼ cup diced avocado, Vinaigrette
    Dressing
Rock Cornish Hens Parmesan
Artichoke Soufflé
½ cup slivered raw celery and carrots with Mint Dressing
½ cup fresh strawberries
demitasse

Friday

LUNCH

Onion Torte
½ cup baked cherry tomatoes
iceberg lettuce with ¼ cup slivered fresh pineapple, no
    dressing necessary
coffee or tea

DINNER

hot fresh artichoke, with Mint Dressing as dip
4 ounces baked lobster tail with ½ fresh lime for garnish
    and juice
½ cup sautéed fresh mushrooms
½ cup slivered and steamed fresh green beans, sprinkled
    with Parmesan cheese
endive and watercress salad with Vinaigrette Dressing
Lemon Snow Pudding Ring
demitasse

Saturday

LUNCH

2 thin slices cold lean beef, wrapped around ½ cup green
    pepper and finely shredded cabbage slaw
½ cup stewed fresh tomatoes and onions served in a
    ramekin
½ ripe papaya with lime
coffee or tea

1 ounce smoked salmon, sliced very thin, with 1 teaspoon
    capers and 2 thin slices onion
Chicken in Champagne
Dilled Carrots
romaine and escarole salad with Buttermilk Dressing
Raspberry Sponge Pudding
demitasse

Escarole is a lovely salad green and a nice change from lettuce, so use it often in place of lettuce or other greens. The
bleached center is pretty, but use some of the green leaves too;
they contain more minerals.

Third Week

Monday

1 cup clear consommé
2 ounces medium-diced or sliced cold chicken (or turkey or seafood) tossed with broken romaine leaves
½ sliced peeled tomato, ¼ cup diced cucumber, ¼ cup sliced fresh or canned mushrooms, ¼ cup thinly sliced celery, 2 tablespoons Green Herb Dressing
coffee or tea

Any combination salad tossed lightly with a dressing and piled on a large plate rather than in a bowl takes on a special look and does not seem like diet food. Orange or grapefruit sections in place of the tomato make a nice variation. By the way, chilled crystal plates make any salad much more attractive.

DINNER

Green Salad Soup
3 ounces broiled tenderloin of beef
½ cup steamed thinly sliced turnips, heavily parslied
Mushrooms Stuffed with Green Beans
heart of palm with No Calorie Dressing
½ ruby red grapefruit
demitasse

Tuesday

LUNCH

1 cup Consommé Céléstine
2 cups Crudité Salad with 2 ounces julienned chicken or
    seafood
coffee or tea

DINNER

1 small, canned, chilled Iceland trout with mustardy
    Yogurt Dressing
Lemon Roasted Lamb
½ cup puréed carrots
½ cup puréed yellow squash
½ cup puréed spinach
1 ounce Cheddar cheese with ½ apple
demitasse

When I serve puréed vegetables I arrange them in rows on a small platter and sprinkle them lavishly with finely minced parsley. They look pretty, so they taste good.

[32]

Wednesday

LUNCH

Artichokes Stuffed with Crabmeat
skewered fresh pineapple, green pepper, and cherry
    tomatoes, broiled for 5 minutes on each side
coffee or tea

DINNER

cold asparagus salad with Vinaigrette Dressing
Veal Loin Florentine
Green Beans Polonaise
Tarragon Tomatoes
Frozen Orange Bowl
demitasse

Thursday

LUNCH

6 large garlic-broiled shrimp, piled in a coquille. Looks like
    more!
3 slender stalks fresh broccoli, sprinkled with Parmesan
    cheese
soft lettuce with Vinaigrette Dressing
any fresh fruit
coffee or tea

Hot shrimp is much more satisfying as an entrée than cold
shrimp, which is so often just an hors d'oeuvre. If you do not

like garlic, skip it and use soy sauce or fresh ginger or just lemon juice. However, garlic does give shrimp a lift.

DINNER

Bibb, red lettuce, and spinach salad with Green Herb
   Dressing
Breast of Chicken Piquante
½ cup steamed green beans with grated orange peel
½ cup fresh mushrooms sautéed in sherry
Apple Sherbet
demitasse

Friday

LUNCH

Crab and Almond Soufflé
2 ounces broiled pineapple fingers rubbed with curry
½ cup steamed fresh okra with grated lemon peel
coffee or tea

Substitute chicken or turkey or any cooked fish for the crab. Bake in individual ramekins or casseroles. Crab and pineapple have a special affinity for each other, and okra likes crab.

DINNER

Iced Roquefort Soup
Red Snapper with Grapefruit
Zucchini Cups
Turnip Pudding
spinach and carrot salad with mustardy Yogurt Dressing
Strawberry Buttermilk Sherbet
demitasse

The new electric ice-cream freezers (Salton, for example) plug into your freezer and do all the work, permitting you to have homemade ice cream and frozen yogurt with little effort on your part.

Saturday

LUNCH

4 ounces fresh carrot juice
1 cup sliced fresh fruit in soft lettuce heart, with 2 ounces
    cottage cheese whipped with grated orange peel
coffee or tea

DINNER

½ cup cold Cucumber Yogurt Soup dusted with dill weed,
    dried or fresh
Fruited Breast of Chicken
Zucchini fan with sautéed onions and tomatoes
watercress, fresh mushroom, and riced egg white salad with
    Sherry French Dressing
Low-Calorie Cheesecake with 1 tablespoon puréed fresh
    fruit sauce (I like raspberries)
demitasse

Fourth Week

Monday

LUNCH

Swiss Cheese Soufflé
½ cup mushrooms sautéed in sherry
Florentine Tomatoes
coffee or tea

DINNER

Stuffed Flounder
½ cup minted green beans and scallions
½ cup sautéed cucumbers, parslied
½ cup julienned endive and hard-cooked egg white with
    Sherry French Dressing
½ cup diced fresh fruit with grated orange peel, served
    over crushed ice
demitasse

[36]

Tuesday

Papaya and Shrimp Salad
3 stalks cold fresh asparagus with Mimosa Dressing
½ cup minted honeydew melon balls
coffee or tea

DINNER

Filet of Beef with Lobster Tail
Stir-fried Vegetables
bowl of raw relishes in ice, served with Buttermilk
    Dressing for dip. A good combination of vegetables is:
    Brussels sprouts, thin slices of white turnip, cucumber
    fingers, cherry tomatoes, raw mushrooms, and Jerusalem
    artichoke slices. Place bowl in a basket lined with a
    brightly colored napkin.
½ cup Watermelon Sherbet in cantaloupe
coffee or tea

Wednesday

LUNCH

Shrimp Creole
Celery with Mustard Sauce, chilled
½ cup fresh strawberries with puréed strawberries spilled
    over them for added flavor
coffee or tea

½ cup jellied madrilène with 1 teaspoon caviar
Breast of Chicken Dublin Style
½ cup steamed, julienned parsnips, heavily parslied
Dilled Carrots
½ cup grated radishes and carrots marinated in Vinaigrette
   Dressing and served on 1 slice Chinese cabbage
Hot Apricot Whip
demitasse

The most bland vegetable is improved with finely chopped parsley sprinkled generously over it. Keep a container in your refrigerator and use it. Chop the parsley very fine in a blender or food processor or by hand; squeeze out excess moisture with a paper towel. It will keep for days in a covered container, but it must be dry. Add chives, mint, or any fresh herb and citrus fruit gratings for a change of flavor and no calories.

Thursday

LUNCH

tossed chicken and fruit salad. For example: ¼ cup orange
   sections; 5 seedless grapes cut in half; ¼ small banana,
   sliced; ½ cup diced fresh pineapple; 2 ounces julienned
   cold chicken; 2 cups broken lettuce; 1 tablespoon, or
   more, chopped parsley. Toss lightly with 1 tablespoon
   Sherry French Dressing or 2 tablespoons strawberry
   yogurt (low-calorie plain yogurt flavored with puréed
   strawberries).
coffee or tea

Mushroom and Endive Salad
2 ounces lean boiled beef and ¼ head cabbage with 2
    tablespoons horseradishy Cottage Cheese Mousse
½ cup whipped steamed yellow squash
½ cup whipped steamed white turnips
Coffee Sponge
demitasse

The thinner you slice meat of any kind, the larger the serving
looks. More tender too.

Friday

LUNCH

Spanish Eggs
Salade Piquante
coffee or tea

Keep the Spanish sauce in a covered container in the refrigerator for a quick lunch idea with a sassy flavor.

DINNER

Cold Lemon Soup
4 ounces grilled filet of salmon with lemon shell cup of
    capers. Decorate with steamed sliced cucumbers, no
    calories.
layered steamed vegetables — pearl onions, celery hearts,
    snipped green beans
red lettuce and grapefruit salad with Green Herb Dressing
1 ounce frozen persimmon
coffee or tea

Persimmons are in the markets for only a short time. Freeze them when they are very ripe. Slice them frozen and serve with a lemon tulip.

Saturday

LUNCH

The favorite Greenhouse Saturday lunch is Oriental Chicken Salad. It's not like any chicken salad you've ever tasted!
coffee or tea

DINNER

Watercress Soup
Roast Veal with Oranges
½ cup salsify, heated in skim milk
½ cup steamed, thinly sliced yellow squash and zucchini, heavily parslied
soft lettuce and 1 tablespoon avocado with No Calorie Dressing
Pear Sherbet
demitasse

Sundays

For dieters, the American tradition of having Sunday dinner at midday is an excellent idea. Your midday meal will take up some time pleasantly, and you won't be as hungry later in the day. It is a good idea to save a new book that promises to be fascinating, or a special section of the Sunday newspaper, for the time of day when you are apt to become restless.

After a big Sunday dinner at noon, you will need only a light meal at night. However, if you prefer, you may switch these menus around and have the supper suggestions for lunch and the heavier meal in the evening. Sunday is the seventh day, you know, and people should do as they please. Preparation for these menus is not complicated and much can be done the day before.

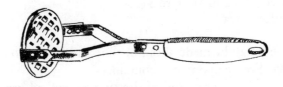

DINNER

thin slice of honeydew melon with 1 slice Prosciutto
2 ounces sliced, broiled lean sirloin steak, natural juices
½ cup cooked mixed vegetables
1 baked tomato
salad of everything green with Green Herb Dressing
Wine Jelly Parfait
coffee or tea

SUPPER OR LUNCH

Green Chile Torte
tomato and celery salad with Green Herb Dressing
Stewed Apples with mandarin oranges
coffee or tea

❧

DINNER

1 ounce lump crabmeat with 1 teaspoon cocktail sauce
3 ounces roasted rib eye of beef, natural juices
¼ cup salsify heated in meat juices
4 stalks asparagus with mint sauce
marinated, chilled fresh artichoke
Cold Lemon Soufflé with ¼ cup mandarin oranges
coffee or tea

SUPPER OR LUNCH

Clear Tomato Soup
Veal en Gelée (make on Saturday)
Green Beans in Mustard Sauce
coffee or tea

The soup may be made ahead of time and frozen to use when
you like. Freeze in one-cup containers.

When adding any kind of dressing to cooked green beans,

[42]

add it just before serving; longer marination sometimes turns them an unattractive gray.

❧

DINNER

½ cup jellied madrilène with orange twist (you may use the canned kind)
Chicken Breast in Foil
Carrots and Yellow Squash
Green Beans Polonaise
celery hearts on ice
Vanilla Ice Cream on ½ cup strawberries
demitasse

SUPPER OR LUNCH

Sunday is a good soup day and gumbo may be made the day before, except for adding the shrimp and okra if you are fussy about your shrimp and okra not being overdone.

Seafood Gumbo
Bibb lettuce with ½ avocado, served with capers and 1 teaspoon lemon juice and oil dressing
Grape Ice
coffee or tea

❧

DINNER

1 demitasse Curried Yogurt Soup
Squab in White Wine
½ cup mushrooms sautéed in juices from roasting
Ratatouille (make Friday or Saturday)
fresh spinach and grapefruit salad with oil and vinegar dressing
Old-Fashioned Prune Whip with 1 tablespoon Soft Custard
coffee or tea

SUPPER OR LUNCH

½ cup Cottage Cheese Mousse ring with ½ cup cold shrimp
    marinated in Vinaigrette Dressing
½ tomato and ½ orange, served on escarole with Sherry
    French Dressing
coffee or tea

❧

DINNER

3 thin slices melon with lime
Chicken with Chanterelles
¼ cup steamed, julienned parsnips, parslied
½ cup steamed broccoli with grated lemon
¼ cup snow pea salad with Sesame Dressing
1 ounce Jarlsberg cheese, 2 toasted water crackers
coffee or tea

SUPPER OR LUNCH

Oyster Bisque
Niçoise Salad
coffee or tea

PART III

RECIPES

Soups

Soups can be satisfying and interesting without providing too many calories and are especially handy for quick and easy preparation. Before dinner or for a snack, serve a demitasse; as part of a meal, a half cup.

Curried Yogurt Soup

FOR FOUR

1 cup (¼ L) plain yogurt, low calorie
1 cup (¼ L) beef broth
½ clove garlic, crushed
½ tsp. or more curry powder
2 medium cooked shrimp, chopped
chopped parsley or chives for garnish

Blend yogurt, broth, garlic and curry powder in blender or food processor. Chill. You may keep this refrigerated for days. Garnish with shrimp and parsley or chives just before serving. Vary by adding diced raw celery and cucumber, or by using cold diced chicken instead of shrimp. Or omit the curry and add 1 cup chopped peeled seeded tomato or spinach with a little onion.

Recommended portion: 1 demitasse; 2½ ounces (26 calories).

Clear Tomato Soup

FOR FOUR

No doubt about it, this is the most popular pick-me-up at The Greenhouse.

> 1 tbsp. margarine
> ¼ cup (½ dL) celery, finely diced
> ¼ cup (½ dL) carrots, finely diced
> ¼ cup (½ dL) onion, finely diced
> 4 parsley sprigs
> 2 cups (½ L) canned tomato juice
> 3 cloves, whole
> 1 bay leaf
> pinch of thyme
> vegetable salt to taste
> white pepper to taste
> 1 cup (¼ L) beef or chicken consommé

Melt margarine, add vegetables, and sauté until soft. Add remaining ingredients, except consommé. Bring to a boil. Cover and simmer for 1 hour. Strain, add consommé, reheat, and serve hot.

Add 1½ tablespoons melted plain gelatin to hot liquid for jellied tomato consommé or molded salad.

Recommended portion: 1 cup (63 calories).

Oyster Bisque

1 tbsp. margarine
½ clove garlic, minced
3 tbsps. onion, chopped
¼ tsp. paprika or curry
8 oz. (¼ L) oysters, chopped
2 cups (½ L) skim milk, hot
vegetable salt to taste
1 tbsp. dry sherry
1 tbsp. chopped parsley
pinch of thyme

Melt margarine, add garlic, onions, and spice, and sauté until yellow. Add oysters and sauté at medium heat until they curl. Add milk. Season. Cover and let stand over a pan of hot water for at least 15 minutes so mixture will cook slowly and not curdle. Ignite sherry, add to milk mixture, and stir in chopped parsley and thyme.

Recommended portion: ½ cup (70 calories).

Variation: Use 1 cup finely diced raw shrimp in place of oysters.

Cucumber Yogurt Soup

FOR EIGHT

This refreshing and attractive soup will be a favorite whether you are dieting or not. Keep some made up in your refrigerator for pick-me-ups. If you're not dieting, add diced avocado, caviar, or seafood with a dollop of sour cream.

2 cups (½ L) yogurt, low calorie
1 cucumber, seeded and finely diced
2 tsp. lemon juice
2 cups (½ L) cold water
¼ cup (½ dL) currants
¼ cup (½ dL) fresh mint, finely chopped
vegetable salt to taste
cracked pepper to taste

Mix yogurt, cucumber, lemon juice, and water in blender or food processor until smooth. Stir in currants and fresh mint by hand. Season and refrigerate. Serve very cold with a thin slice of cucumber floating on top.
Recommended portion: ½ cup (19 calories).

Seafood Gumbo

FOR SIX

1 slice bacon
¼ cup (½ dL) onion, finely diced
¼ cup (½ dL) green pepper, finely diced
1 cup (¼ L) celery, finely diced
2 cups (½ L) fresh or canned tomatoes, finely chopped
3 cups (¾ L) chicken broth
1 cup (¼ L) uncooked, peeled shrimp
1 cup (¼ L) fresh, frozen, or canned crabmeat
2 cups (½ L) okra, fresh or frozen
¼ cup (½ dL) chopped parsley
vegetable salt to taste
filé seasoning to taste (optional)

Dice bacon (freezing it makes this easier) and sauté it in the pot you will make the soup in. Add onion, green pepper, and celery. Sauté until yellow, not brown. Add tomatoes and chicken broth. Cook until all vegetables are soft. Add shrimp, crabmeat, okra, and parsley. Cover, and cook 5 minutes. Season. Add filé if desired, but not until ready to serve. If you add filé too soon, the gumbo will be stringy.

Recommended portion: 1 cup (75 calories).

Rice and gumbo go with each other. For a full meal pour gumbo over ½ cup cooked converted rice (111 calories).

Clam and Mushroom Soup

FOR SIX

3 cups (¾ L) chicken broth
¼ cup (½ dL) onion, thinly sliced
1 cup (¼ L) minced clams
½ cup (1 dL) canned, fresh or dried mushrooms, thinly sliced
a few bean threads or rain noodles
2 tbsp. chopped parsley
vegetable salt to taste

Put broth, onions, clams, and mushrooms in a pot and bring to a boil. Cover and boil 1 minute. Add bean threads and cook until transparent. Add parsley and season. Bean threads may be purchased at good food markets or Oriental food shops.

Recommended portion: ¾ cup (41 calories).

Watercress Soup

FOR FOUR

2 cups (½ L) chicken broth
1 cup (¼ L) watercress leaves
¼ cup (½ dL) green onion, thinly sliced
vegetable salt to taste
4 thin slices of lemon

Blend watercress and onion in blender with ½ cup broth. Remove to saucepan. Add rest of broth, cover, and bring to a boil. Simmer for 1 minute. Season to taste. Serve hot with slice of lemon.

Recommended portion: ½ cup (17 calories).

Variation: Add 2 teaspoons softened gelatin to hot liquid. Cool and serve jellied.

Cold Lemon Soup

FOR FOUR

2 cups (½ L) chicken broth
1 egg
1 tbsp. lemon juice
1 tsp. grated lemon rind
½ cup (1 dL) skim milk
pinch of cayenne pepper
vegetable salt to taste
chopped parsley or chives for garnish

Heat broth to a boil; beat in egg, lemon juice, and rind. Add milk. Cook 1 minute. Season. Cool. Serve very cold with chopped parsley or chives.

Recommended portion: ½ cup (44 calories).

Consommé Céléstine

2 cups (½ L) chicken broth
¼ cup (½ dL) green onion, sliced paper thin
1 egg white, slightly beaten
vegetable salt to taste
a few drops soy sauce
2 tbsps. chopped parsley

Bring broth and onions to a boil for 1 minute. Stir in egg white with a fork. Add seasonings and parsley.
    Recommended portion: ½ cup (12 calories).

Vegetable Chowder

½ cup (1 dL) carrots, finely diced
½ cup (1 dL) yellow squash, finely diced
½ cup (1 dL) celery, finely diced
½ cup (1 dL) green beans, finely diced
¼ cup (½ dL) onion, thinly sliced
1 tbsp. whipped margarine
2 cups (½ L) skim milk
vegetable salt to taste
chopped parsley

Blanch carrots, squash, celery, and green beans for 1 minute. Drain. Sauté onions in margarine until soft, not brown. Add milk and vegetables. Cover and simmer for 5 minutes. Season and sprinkle with chopped parsley or your favorite fresh herb. Serve hot.
    Recommended portion: 1 cup (81 calories).

Jellied Vegetable Consommé

FOR FOUR

2 cups (½ L) jellied beef consommé
¼ cup (½ dL) seeded cucumber, finely diced
1 cup (¼ L) tomato, peeled, seeded, finely chopped
¼ cup (½ dL) green onion, sliced paper thin
½ cup (1 dL) celery, finely diced
1 tsp. salad oil
1 tbsp. red wine vinegar
twist of lemon for garnish

Lightly mix all ingredients. Refrigerate. Serve with twist of lemon.
Recommended portion: ½ cup (40 calories).

Beet and Yogurt Soup

FOR FOUR

1 cup (¼ L) plain yogurt, low calorie
¼ cup (½ dL) cooked or canned beets, chopped fine
1 cooked egg white, chopped fine
¼ cup (½ dL) cooked shrimp, chopped
¼ cup (½ dL) cucumber, chopped fine
⅛ tsp. dried dill weed
4 ice cubes
4 slices of lemon for garnish

In a bowl, mix all ingredients except lemon slices. Chill. Serve with lemon slices floating on top.
Recommended portion: ⅓ cup (44 calories).

Minted Pea Soup

1 tsp. whipped margarine
¼ cup (½ dL) onion, finely diced
1½ cups (3½ dL) chicken broth
1½ cups (3½ dL) frozen peas
2 lettuce leaves, iceberg or romaine
¼ cup (½ dL) parsley sprigs
a few leaves of fresh mint
1 cup (¼ L) skim milk
chopped chives or grated orange peel for garnish

Melt margarine, add onion and ½ cup chicken broth. Cook over medium heat until onions are soft. Add peas, lettuce, parsley, and mint. Cover and boil for 2 minutes. Add remaining broth and bring to a boil. Remove from heat and cool. Put in a blender or food processor and blend until smooth. Add milk. Chill. Serve garnished with chopped chives or grated orange peel for zest. Good hot also.

Recommended portion: 1 demitasse (25 calories).

Green Salad Soup

FOR FOUR

2½ cups (6 dL) chicken broth
1 egg, beaten
¼ cup (½ dL) chopped raw spinach
2 tbsps. watercress leaves
1 tbsp. chopped chives
2 tbsps. chopped parsley
4 sliced green onions (white part only)
vegetable salt to taste

Heat broth to a boil. Pour egg in slowly, stirring with a fork. Add greens and onions. Season. Cover and cook 3 minutes. Serve at once.

Recommended portion: ½ cup (29 calories).

Carrot Soup

FOR SIX

½ cup (1 dL) onion, thinly sliced
2 cups (½ L) carrots, scraped and diced
1 cup (¼ L) chicken broth
2 cups (½ L) skim milk
¼ cup (½ dL) apple, peeled and diced
1 tsp. vegetable salt
¼ cup (½ dL) avocado, mashed
a few drops of hot pepper sauce

Put onions, carrots, and broth in a saucepan. Cover and cook until carrots are tender, but not soft. Add milk and apple. Cool. Blend in food processor or blender. Season. Serve garnished with avocado and seasoned with hot pepper sauce. Serve hot or cold.

Recommended portion: ½ cup soup (59 calories); 1 teaspoon avocado (6 calories).

Iced Roquefort Soup

½ cup (1 dL) crumbled Roquefort cheese
8 ice cubes
2 tbsps. chopped parsley
2 tbsps. chopped green onion (white part only)
2 cups (½ L) yogurt, low calorie

Put cheese, ice cubes, parsley, and onion in blender or food processor. Whip until smooth. Add yogurt and mix until blended. Serve cold. You may add a few bits of cooked shrimp or caviar for a more elegant soup.

Recommended portion: ½ cup (90 calories).

Variation: Add 1 tablespoon unflavored melted gelatin for a molded salad to serve with beef.

Quick Borscht

1 10½-oz. (285 g) can beef consommé
1 1-pound (450 g) can beets and juice
½ cup (1 dL) sliced onion
juice of one lemon

Combine everything in blender. Serve cold.

Recommended portion: ½ cup (35 calories).

Potassium Bouillon

Everyone is concerned with nutritional values today, or should be. This Greenhouse pick-me-up is full of minerals, but loses vitamins because of long cooking. It has so few calories that you don't have to worry about them.

1 cup (¼ L) carrot peelings
1 cup (¼ L) green beans, asparagus, or zucchini
a few mushroom stems, if you have them
a few stalks of celery, with leaves
1 cup (¼ L) any vegetable peelings
1 onion, sliced
a handful of spinach, watercress, parsley, or a combination
    of all three

Cover everything with cold water. Bring to a boil, then simmer at low heat for 1 hour. Strain, season the broth, and drink hot or cold. This is merely an outline. Use any vegetable, including thin skins of potatoes. At The Greenhouse we use the discards from vegetable preparations, outside pieces of lettuce, cabbage, etc., not leftovers from service, as we explained to a nervous guest.

Salads and
Their Dressings

Antipasto Salad

FOR FOUR

1 medium green pepper
1 medium red onion, thinly sliced
3 tbsps. Vinaigrette Dressing
12 spears cooked or canned asparagus
1 cup (¼ L) cooked, slivered celery
1 tomato, peeled
1 cup (¼ L) sliced cucumber
16 canned mushrooms
several leaves of red lettuce
16 cooked, medium-size shrimp
2 hard-cooked eggs, sliced
chopped parsley for garnish

Place green pepper under broiler until skin is blistered. Remove and peel off skins. Lazy? Blanch 1 minute in boiling water. Cut in thin strips. Marinate overnight, with the onion, in 1 tablespoon Vinaigrette Dressing. Sprinkle 2 tablespoons Vinaigrette Dressing over the asparagus, celery, tomato, cucumber, and mushrooms and refrigerate for a few hours. Drain.

Place red lettuce leaves on a serving tray and add all the drained ingredients in an attractive arrangement. Top with shrimp and eggs, and sprinkle with chopped parsley. All guests serve themselves. If you would like to substitute or add freshly cooked green beans, marinate them for a short time at room temperature. They will not change into that dismal gray green you encounter when they have been refrigerated in the dressing.

Recommended portion: ¼ of salad (123 calories).

Crudité Salad

FOR FOUR

Very, very good for lunch with 2 ounces of cold meat or seafood.

  3 stalks asparagus, sliced diagonally
  ½ cup (1 dL) green beans, sliced diagonally
  ¼ cup (½ dL) cauliflower buds
  ¼ cup (½ dL) celery, slivered
  1 small zucchini or yellow squash, sliced thin
  1 qt. (1 L) boiling water
  ½ cup (1 dL) fresh mushrooms, sliced thin
  ½ small cucumber, sliced paper thin
  ¼ cup (½ dL) green onions, sliced diagonally
  1 medium tomato, peeled and quartered
  5 radishes, sliced thin
  1 cup (¼ L) Belgian endive or romaine lettuce, broken
    into chunks
  chopped parsley or chives for garnish

This is merely a guide. You may make this salad with any uncooked vegetables. It is an excellent clean-out-the-refrigerator salad. I usually slice the vegetables on the diagonal, because I like them that way. Put the asparagus, green beans, cauliflower, celery, and squash in a bowl. Cover with *boiling* water for 1 minute. Drain and cool. Add rest of ingredients. Cover with plastic wrap or foil, punch one tiny hole in it, and refrigerate until ready to use. Then add 1 cup Vinaigrette or Sherry French Dressing and refrigerate for 30 minutes to 1 hour. Drain all the dressing off. Serve on very cold plates and sprinkle with chopped parsley or chives.

Recommended portions: ½ cup for dinner salad (78 calories); 1½ cups for luncheon entrée (234 calories).

Variation: You may marinate with any oil and vinegar dressing you wish, for as long as you wish, then drain by putting the salad in a sieve over a bowl. Keep the dressing and use it again and again; the flavor improves each time.

Mushroom and Endive Salad

FOR FOUR

8 large fresh mushrooms
2 tbsps. lemon juice
2 heads Belgian endive, slivered
½ cup (1 dL) celery, slivered
1 tbsp. chives
1 tbsp. safflower oil
½ tsp. vegetable salt
1 bunch watercress, trimmed
cracked pepper to taste

Wash mushrooms in cold water. Pat dry with a paper towel. Slice very thin. Pour lemon juice over them. Add the endive, celery, chives, oil, and vegetable salt. Toss lightly with watercress and pepper.

Recommended portion: ½ cup (40 calories).

Variation: Substitute 1 cup fresh spinach for the endive, and half a thinly sliced red apple (with skin) for the mushrooms.

Celery with Mustard Sauce

FOR FOUR

8 stalks celery
¼ cup (½ dL) yogurt, low calorie
2 tsps. Dijon mustard
1 tsp. lemon juice
2 tbsps. chopped parsley
vegetable salt to taste

Strip as many strings as possible from the celery. Slice thin on the bias. Steam 2 minutes. Cover with ice water to cool quickly. Mix yogurt, mustard, lemon juice, and parsley. Toss with celery and season. Serve on fresh spinach leaves or lettuce or serve warm as a vegetable.

Recommended portion: ¼ cup (14 calories).

Variation: For Green Beans in Mustard Sauce, substitute 1 cup fresh beans for the celery.

Niçoise Salad

¼ head crisp lettuce
2 tbsps. water-packed tuna fish
¼ cup (½ dL) celery, blanched and thinly sliced
¼ cup (½ dL) red onion, sliced thin
1 egg white, hard-cooked
1 small tomato, peeled and quartered
½ cup (1 dL) green beans, cooked and chilled
1 tbsp. chopped parsley
a pinch thyme
a pinch rosemary
fresh ground pepper
1 tbsp. Vinaigrette Dressing

Arrange lettuce leaves in a bowl or on a plate. Add tuna fish, celery, onion, sliced egg white, tomato, and beans. Sprinkle with herbs. Dribble Vinaigrette Dressing over salad. You may add an anchovy or two if you like, without causing a disaster to your diet regime.

Total calories: 200.

Salade Piquante

FOR FOUR

This is a variation of the famous Cobb salad of Brown Derby fame. Use it for lunch with a julienne of chicken or any lean meat or seafood. It is a favorite dinner salad and easy to handle on a buffet where everyone helps herself.

2 cups (½ L) romaine lettuce, chopped
2 slices crisp bacon, crumbled
1 hard-cooked egg white, finely diced
2 tomatoes, peeled, seeded, finely chopped
¼ cup (½ dL) avocado, chopped
2 tbsps. pimiento, finely diced
1 tbsp. Roquefort cheese, crumbled
¼ cup (½ dL) chopped parsley
2 tbsps. Pear Vinegar Dressing

Put lettuce in bottom of salad bowl. Arrange each of the chopped ingredients on top in a pattern — the spokes of a wheel, for example. Chill. Add dressing just before serving.

Recommended portion: 1 cup (121 calories).

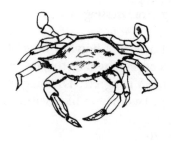

Celery Root Salad

Fresh celery root in the market isn't pretty to look at, but it makes a lovely salad. (You can also purchase it in a can.)

Wash and peel the root. Cut in julienne pieces and steam or boil until tender in water to which a little lemon juice has been added. Drain, and cool by pouring ice water over it. Drain well. Add 3 tablespoons (145 ml) white wine vinegar and chill. When ready to use, drain and toss with Vinaigrette Dressing.

Recommended portion: 2 tablespoons with lettuce (10 calories); 1 teaspoon Vinaigrette Dressing (adds 18 calories).

Crabmeat and Grapefruit Salad

1 head romaine
1 lb. (450 g) lump crabmeat
2 grapefruit, peeled
¼ cup (½ dL) catsup
½ cup (1 dL) yogurt
2 tbsps. lemon juice
1 tbsp. horseradish
1 bunch watercress, trimmed, for garnish

Divide romaine into four servings and place in center of plates. Section the grapefruit and arrange on the lettuce. Put ¼ pound crabmeat in the middle of each plate. Mix catsup, yogurt, lemon juice, and horseradish, and spoon 1 tablespoonful over each salad. Decorate with watercress.

Recommended portion: ¼ of salad (203 calories).

Artichokes Stuffed with Crabmeat

FOR FOUR

4 artichokes
1 tbsp. lemon juice
2 tsps. vegetable salt
½ cup (1 dL) Red Wine Vinegar Dressing
2 cups (½ L) lump crabmeat
½ cup (1 dL) Yogurt Dressing with horseradish

Trim stem of each artichoke. Pull off tough leaves at base. Cut off top third and spread each artichoke open. Dig out center fuzzy portion with a spoon or grapefruit knife. Place in a deep saucepan. Add boiling water, lemon juice, and salt, to cover. Cover and cook 30 minutes or until a leaf pulls out easily. Remove and drain. Fit snugly in a bowl and pour Red Wine Vinegar Dressing over. Marinate for several hours or overnight. Remove from marinade and fill each artichoke with ½ cup of crabmeat. Chill. Serve with horseradishy Yogurt Dressing (2 tablespoons is plenty for you).

Recommended portion: 1 stuffed artichoke (133 calories).

Papaya and Shrimp Salad

FOR ONE

lettuce or watercress for garnish
½ ripe papaya, seeded
3½ oz. (100 g) baby shrimp
1 tbsp. finely grated fresh coconut
½ tsp. fresh lime juice
⅛ tsp. grated fresh ginger root
1 slice of lime

Place papaya on bed of lettuce or watercress. Mix shrimp, coconut, lime juice, and ginger root and pile in cavity of papaya. Decorate with lime slice cut halfway through to center and twist.

Total calories: 190.

Watercress and Potato Salad

FOR FOUR

1 potato
1 bunch watercress
¼ cup (½ dL) green onion, sliced thin
2 tbsps. Vinaigrette Dressing
vegetable salt to taste
cracked pepper to taste

Boil potato in skin. Cool and peel. Slice thin. Trim watercress
of stems and toss with the potato, onion, and dressing. Correct seasoning.

Recommended portion: ¼ cup (49 calories).

Vinaigrette Dressing

Use for marinating vegetables, seafood, and greens.

1 tbsp. Dijon mustard
2 tbsps. lemon juice
2 tbsps. vinegar
⅜ cup (¾ dL) safflower oil
vegetable salt to taste
½ tsp. freshly ground pepper
⅜ cup (¾ dL) water

Put first six ingredients in a bowl and beat for 1 minute with
a whisk. Whip in the water a little at a time.

Recommended portion: 1 tablespoon (54 calories).

Variations: For Mimosa Dressing, add one hard-cooked
egg white, finely diced or sieved, and 2 tablespoons finely
chopped parsley. For Niçoise Dressing, add ½ clove garlic,
minced; 2 tablespoons onion, minced; and 2 tablespoons
chopped parsley.

Sherry French Dressing

1 egg
¼ tsp. sugarless sweetener
½ tsp. vegetable salt
1 cup (¼ L) safflower oil
¼ cup (½ dL) cider vinegar
¼ cup (½ dL) dry sherry
1 cup water
1 clove garlic, crushed

Beat egg lightly with sweetener and salt. Add oil alternately with vinegar, beating with a whisk. Dribble sherry and water in slowly, beating constantly. Add garlic. Keeps well in refrigerator and complements any salad.

Recommended portion for 1 small salad: 1 tablespoon (50 calories).

Any salad dressing can be diluted with cold water for further calorie cutting.

Red Wine Vinegar Dressing

¼ cup (½ dL) water
¼ cup (½ dL) red wine vinegar
¼ cup (½ dL) safflower oil
1 tsp. Dijon mustard
2 tsps. prepared horseradish
1 clove garlic, minced
2 tbsps. chopped parsley

"The better the red wine vinegar, the better the dressing" (Fauchon said this, I think). Mix all ingredients thoroughly. Especially good for marinating fresh artichokes.

Recommended portion: 1 tablespoon (45 calories).

Green Herb Dressing

A favorite for both seafood and green salads. Some guests order it at every meal.

¼ cup (½ dL) parsley
¼ cup (½ dL) watercress leaves
4 green onions
1 tsp. dry mustard
¼ cup (½ dL) water
1 egg yolk
¼ cup (½ dL) safflower oil
¼ cup (½ dL) tarragon vinegar
½ tsp. dried mixed salad herbs
½ tsp. horseradish, prepared

Mix all ingredients in blender or by hand with a whisk.
Recommended portion: 1 tablespoon (32 calories).

Buttermilk Dressing

1 cup (¼ L) buttermilk
1 cup (¼ L) cottage cheese, low fat
1 tbsp. onion, chopped
½ clove garlic, crushed
2 tbsps. lemon juice
vegetable salt to taste
1 tsp. chives (optional)

Mix all ingredients together in blender.
Recommended portion: 1 tablespoon (9 calories).
Variation: Add 2 ounces Roquefort or blue cheese. (1 tablespoon has 13 calories.)

[69]

Pear Vinegar Dressing

I especially like this dressing on Salade Piquante.

   ¼ cup (½ dL) pear vinegar
   ½ cup (1 dL) safflower oil
   1 tsp. lemon juice
   1 clove garlic
   vegetable salt to taste
   fresh-ground pepper to taste

Mix oil, vinegar, and lemon juice with a whisk. Crush garlic and add. Season to your taste.
   Recommended portion: 1 teaspoon (24 calories).
   Pear vinegar is a Harry and David product which can be found in good grocery stores. If it's unavailable, you can substitute white wine vinegar.

No Calorie Dressing

   ½ cup (1 dL) wine vinegar
   ½ tsp. vegetable salt
   ½ clove garlic, crushed
   1 tbsp. chopped parsley
   a pinch of oregano, tarragon, or curry

Mix well.
   Recommended portion: 1 tablespoon (2 calories).

Sesame Dressing

⅜ cup (¾ dL) water
⅜ cup (¾ dL) safflower oil
3 tbsps. vinegar
2 tbsps. lemon juice
½ tsp. sugar substitute
½ tsp. salt
1 tsp. sesame seeds, toasted golden brown

Mix together in a bowl. Serve on freshly cooked vegetables, especially snow peas.

Recommended portion: 1 tablespoon (44 calories).

Mint Dressing

½ cup (1 dL) safflower oil
¼ cup (½ dL) red wine vinegar
½ cup (1 dL) fresh mint leaves, minced
1 clove garlic, crushed
½ tsp. cracked pepper
1½ tsps. vegetable salt

Mix together. This is good marinade for fresh artichokes or other vegetables, served hot or cold.

Recommended portion: 1 teaspoon for ½ cup vegetables (9 calories); 1 tablespoon for 1 artichoke (27 calories).

Cottage Cheese Dressing

1 cup (¼ L) low-fat cottage cheese, loosely packed
2 tbsps. honey
1 tsp. grated orange peel
1 tbsp. lemon juice

Mix in blender or food processor until smooth.
Recommended portion: 1 tablespoon (15 calories).

Yogurt Dressing

2 raw egg yolks
1 tsp. dry mustard or horseradish
2 egg yolks, hard-cooked and pressed through sieve
2 cups (½ L) yogurt
2 tsps. lemon juice
vegetable salt

Mix raw egg yolks with mustard or horseradish and add to cooked egg yolks. Beat in rest of ingredients slowly.
Recommended portion: 1 tablespoon (16 calories).

Cheese and Eggs

Swiss Cheese Soufflé

FOR FOUR

2 tbsps. whipped margarine
3 tbsps. flour
¾ cup (1¾ dL) skim milk, hot
½ tsp. prepared mustard
a pinch of cayenne pepper
4 drops of hot pepper sauce
1 tsp. vegetable salt
1 cup (¼ L) grated Swiss cheese
4 egg yolks, beaten
6 egg whites, beaten stiff

Melt margarine, stir in flour, and cook until bubbly. Add milk and seasonings. Boil for 1 minute, stirring constantly. Remove from heat and stir in cheese. Add beaten egg yolks. Let mixture cool. Stir ⅓ of beaten egg whites into mixture and fold in the rest. Pour mixture into 1½-quart soufflé dish, lightly greased. Bake at 375°F/190°C for 30 minutes, or until puffed and brown.

Recommended portion: ¼ soufflé (306 calories).

It goes without saying that with a soufflé of this size for lunch, you would serve only a few raw relishes or a lettuce salad.

Crab and Almond Soufflé

FOR EIGHT

This soufflé is usually served on three fingers of broiled, fresh, or water-packed pineapple rubbed with curry, and no sauce is necessary.

¼ cup (½ dL) whipped margarine
⅜ cup (¾ dL) flour
½ tsp. dry mustard
1¼ cups (3 dL) skim milk
3 cups (¾ L) cooked crabmeat, minced
¼ cup (½ dL) blanched almonds, slivered
4 egg yolks, beaten
6 egg whites, beaten stiff

Melt margarine, stir in flour and mustard. Cook until bubbly. Add milk; cook until thickened. Cool slightly and stir in crabmeat, almonds, and yolks. Fold in whites. Pour into lightly greased casserole. Bake at 375°F/190°C for about 35 minutes, or until knife inserted in center comes out clean.

Recommended portion: 1 cup (188 calories).

Variation: Chicken is a good substitute for the crabmeat.

Cheese Custard

FOR FOUR

4 egg yolks
1½ cups (3½ dL) skim milk
1½ cups (3½ dL) grated Swiss cheese
⅛ tsp. nutmeg
vegetable salt to taste

Beat egg yolks, add skim milk, cheese, nutmeg, and salt. Pour into shallow casserole and bake at 350°F/180°C for 30 minutes.

Recommended portion: ¼ casserole (250 calories).

Shrimp and Spinach Quiche

FOR SIX

A most popular lunch.

12 medium shrimp, sliced
½ cup (1 dL) fresh spinach leaves, broken
1 tbsp. onion, finely diced
1 cup (¼ L) Swiss cheese, grated
5 eggs, beaten
2 cups (½ L) skim milk
½ tsp. vegetable salt
a pinch of paprika

Place shrimp, spinach, and onion in lightly oiled 8-inch quiche casserole or pie tin. Sprinkle cheese over top. Combine eggs, milk, and seasonings, and pour over cheese. Bake at 325°F/165°C until set.

Recommended portion: ⅙ of pie (165 calories).
Variation: Substitute crab or lobster for the shrimp, and broccoli or mushrooms for the spinach.

Green Chile Torte

FOR SIX

1½ cups (3½ dL) skim milk
2 eggs
1¼ cups (3 dL) jack cheese, shredded
1 4-oz. can whole green chile peppers, seeded and finely
    diced
¼ tsp. vegetable salt
a pinch of cayenne

Heat milk until hot but not boiling. Beat eggs; slowly beat milk into them. Add cheese, peppers, and seasonings. Pour into 6 lightly greased shirred-egg dishes, or a 9-inch pie tin. Bake at 325°F/165°C about 40 minutes, or until set.
Recommended portion: ⅙ of recipe (111 calories).

Onion Torte

FOR EIGHT

1½ cups (3½ dL) thinly sliced white onions
2 tbsps. whipped margarine
2 cups (½ L) skim milk
4 eggs, beaten
¼ cup (½ dL) grated Swiss cheese
a pinch of nutmeg

Slowly sauté onions in margarine until soft. Heat milk, add eggs and cook gently until mixture coats a spoon. Remove from heat; add onions, cheese, and nutmeg. Pour into 4-ounce ramekins or soufflé dishes. Bake at 350°F/180°C until set. Serve hot.

Recommended portion: 4 ounces (115 calories).

Spanish Eggs

FOR SIX

This recipe makes 3 cups sauce — enough for 12 eggs. Leftover sauce keeps well refrigerated or frozen.

1 tsp. whipped margarine
½ cup (1 dL) sliced onion
1 clove garlic, crushed
½ cup (1 dL) celery, chopped
¼ cup (½ dL) green pepper, sliced
2 cups (½ L) tomatoes, peeled, seeded, and chopped
1 bay leaf
4 cloves
1 tsp. vegetable salt
6 eggs
¼ cup (½ dL) chopped parsley for garnish

Melt margarine, add onion, garlic, celery, and green pepper. Sauté until soft, but do not brown. Add tomatoes, bay leaf, and cloves. Cook until thickened. Add vegetable salt.

Poach eggs, cover with sauce. Sprinkle with parsley. Easy!

Recommended portion: 1 egg and ¼ cup sauce (154 calories).

Cottage Cheese Mousse

1 tbsp. gelatin
¼ cup (½ dL) cold water
2 cups (½ L) cottage cheese
½ cup (1 dL) skim milk
1 tbsp. grated onion
½ tsp. vegetable salt
a pinch of cayenne pepper

Soften gelatin in cold water. Melt over hot water. Whip cheese and milk in blender or food processor to the consistency of whipped cream. Add gelatin, onion, and seasonings. Pour into 1-pint mold and refrigerate until set.

Recommended portion: ½ cup (104 calories).

Variations: Add 1 tablespoon prepared horseradish or mustard. Stir in 1 cup chopped raw vegetables. Use your imagination.

Vegetables

WHILE EVERY MORSEL of food we eat contains calories, vegetables contain fewer than most other foods and are full of necessary vitamins and minerals. Although recommended portions at The Greenhouse vary from ¼ to ½ cup, vegetables are the food you should increase if you find that you need a more substantial diet.

Steam or stir-fry vegetables, keeping them underdone to preserve their flavor, texture, vitamins, and minerals. Invest in a vegetable steamer. You will find yourself and your family enjoying vegetables more. Include both green and yellow vegetables each day.

Carrots and Yellow Squash

FOR FOUR

½ cup (1 dL) water
1 lemon, sliced
½ tsp. sugar substitute
⅛ tsp. cinnamon
1 cup (¼ L) carrots, thinly sliced diagonally
1 cup (¼ L) yellow squash, thinly sliced diagonally
chopped parsley for garnish

Place water, lemon, and sugar substitute in a saucepan and simmer until reduced by half. Add cinnamon. Simmer for 5 minutes. Steam the carrots and the squash until fork tender, about 4 minutes. Add to cinnamon mixture and heat. Sprinkle with chopped parsley.
Recommended portion: ½ cup (24 calories).

Carrots in Vodka

FOR FOUR

1 cup (¼ L) julienne of raw carrots
¼ cup (½ dL) vodka
1 tbsp. slivered orange peel
a pinch of sugar substitute
vegetable salt to taste

Place everything in a small pot. Cover and simmer until carrots are tender.
Recommended portion: ¼ cup (25 calories).

Dilled Carrots

1 cup (¼ L) carrots sliced thin
1 tsp. whipped margarine
a pinch of sugar substitute
½ tsp. vegetable salt
1 tbsp. fresh or 1 tsp. dried dill weed
¼ tsp. cracked pepper

Steam carrots for 4 minutes. Melt margarine in a skillet. Add carrots and remaining ingredients. Cook until thoroughly heated.

Recommended portion: ½ cup (30 calories).

Variation: For Dilled Green Beans, use fresh beans cut diagonally.

Gratin of Celery

2 celery hearts
1 cup (¼ L) chicken or beef broth
1 tbsp. grated Parmesan cheese
2 tbsps. chopped parsley for garnish

Wash celery hearts thoroughly in warm salted water. Remove leaves. Plunge in boiling water for 1 minute. Split each in half, lengthwise. Place in a shallow casserole and pour the broth over. Cover and bake at 350°F/180°C until celery is tender, about 30 minutes. Sprinkle with cheese. Run under broiler to melt. Sprinkle with chopped parsley.

Recommended portion: ½ heart (15 calories).

Green Beans Polonaise

1 lb. (450 g) green beans
1 hard-cooked egg
2 tbsps. chopped parsley
1 tsp. chopped chives or green onion
¼ tsp. vegetable salt

Steam green beans until tender, about 10 minutes. Chop egg or put through a sieve. Mix with the parsley, onion, and vegetable salt. Toss into the beans.

Recommended portion: ½ cup (48 calories).

Zucchini Cups

FOR SIX

2 medium-large zucchini
1 tbsp. whipped margarine
1 cup (¼ L) fresh mushrooms, finely diced
1 tbsp. shallots, or green onion, minced
vegetable salt to taste
1 tbsp. chopped parsley
1 tbsp. grated Parmesan cheese

Cut zucchini in thirds crosswise. Steam for 5 minutes. Cool and stand each piece on end. Dig out center seeds, leaving a thin layer in the bottom. Melt margarine. Add shallots and mushrooms. Sauté 2 minutes. Season and add parsley. Fill cavities of squash with mixture. Sprinkle with cheese. Reheat at 350°F/180°C.

Recommended portion: 1 piece (34 calories).

Zucchini

Bright green zucchini is a great vegetable for dieters. Just slice it thinly, add a little chopped onion, and cook it for five minutes in a covered skillet with very little water. Do yellow squash the same way; or mix the two for a colorful dish.

Zucchini fans are pretty too. Select small squashes and slice them lengthwise, but not all the way: the slices should remain attached at the blossom end. Cook as above. Remove them and spread the slices in a fan shape on the plate. Serve with your favorite sauce, or just lemon juice and fresh-ground pepper.

Recommended portion: ½ cup slices, 9 calories; or 1 zucchini fan, about 20 calories.

Stir-fried Spinach

FOR FOUR

1 lb. (450 g) fresh spinach
1 tsp. whipped margarine
¼ cup (½ dL) onion, thinly sliced
vegetable salt to taste

Wash spinach and remove heavy stems. Drain. Melt margarine in hot skillet. Add onion and stir for 30 seconds. Add spinach and stir for 1 minute. Season.

Recommended portion: ½ cup (33 calories).

Variations: For added flavor sprinkle this with a few grains of Parmesan cheese or grated lemon or orange peel; or substitute a few thinly sliced mushrooms for the onion.

Ratatouille

1 medium zucchini
1 small eggplant, peeled
1 medium tomato, peeled
1 small green pepper
1 tbsp. salad oil
½ cup (¼ L) onion, thinly sliced
2 cloves garlic, minced
1 tsp. vegetable salt
2 tbsps. chopped parsley for garnish

Wash zucchini and eggplant and slice in ¼-inch slices. Cut tomato into medium-sized dice. Seed pepper, blanch 1 minute, and cut in strips.

Heat oil, add onion, and sauté 1 minute. Do not brown. Add tomato and cook 1 minute. Add remaining ingredients except parsley. Cover, bring to boiling point, and simmer 5 minutes. Remove cover and continue simmering until liquid has evaporated. Season and sprinkle with parsley. Serve hot as a vegetable or cold as a salad on fresh spinach leaves.

Recommended portion: ½ cup (50 calories).

Vegetables à la Grecque

FOR FOUR TO SIX

THE MARINADE:

1 cup (¼ L) chicken broth
⅓ cup (¾ dL) dry white wine
5 peppercorns
1 clove garlic, slivered
1 tsp. vegetable salt
6 parsley sprigs
1 bay leaf
2 tbsps. lemon juice
1 tbsp. salad oil

Combine all ingredients in a medium saucepan. Bring to a boil, cover, and simmer 30 minutes. Strain.

THE VEGETABLES:

2 medium onions, cut in quarters
1 medium zucchini, sliced diagonally
1 medium yellow squash, sliced diagonally
1 small green pepper, cut in large dice
1 small sweet red pepper or pimiento, cut in strips
4 tbsps. chopped parsley for garnish

Add onions to strained liquid. Cover and simmer until tender. Add rest of ingredients except parsley. Cover and cook 5 minutes. Pour into a shallow container. Cover and refrigerate overnight. Serve in small ramekins or bowls. Sprinkle with chopped parsley.

Recommended portion: ¼ cup (34 calories).

Variation: For Mushrooms à la Grecque, use 1 pound fresh mushrooms cut in half instead of both squashes.

Turnip Pudding

8 medium white turnips, peeled and sliced
2 tbsps. onion, chopped
½ cup (1 dL) skim milk
vegetable salt, to taste
2 egg whites, beaten stiff

Cook the turnips and onion in a steamer, or covered in boiling water, until just tender. Do not overcook. Drain. Mash, or whip thoroughly in a blender or food processor. Heat milk, add turnips, and cook until milk is absorbed. Cool. Season and fold into the stiffly beaten egg whites. Pour into a lightly buttered casserole and bake at 350°F/180°C until puffy and lightly browned. Or skip the egg whites and serve sprinkled with chopped parsley or chives.

Recommended portion: ½ cup (48 calories).

Variation: Substitute yellow turnips and bake in a scooped-out orange.

Stir-fried Vegetables

FOR SIX

1 tbsp. peanut or vegetable oil
½ cup (1 dL) carrots, slivered
½ cup (1 dL) celery, slivered
1 medium zucchini, thinly sliced diagonally
2 tbsps. chicken broth or water
¼ lb. (115 g) snow peas
vegetable salt to taste

Heat oil in a skillet till very hot. Add carrots and stir-fry for 1 minute. Add celery and zucchini and stir 1 minute. Add chicken broth; cover and cook 30 seconds. Add snow peas; cover and cook 30 seconds more. (If peas are big, add with other vegetables.) Season, stir, and serve at once with or without chopped parsley or a few drops of soy sauce.

Recommended portions: ½ cup (34 calories).

Variation: Any vegetable combination may be used.

Tarragon Tomatoes

FOR SIX

Tomatoes have been included in low-calorie diets for years, and personally I feel they are overworked. They can be more palatable with the addition of herbs and seasonings. This dish is a favorite.

3 ripe tomatoes
1 clove garlic, minced
⅛ tsp. dried tarragon
⅛ tsp. cracked pepper
a few sprinklings of Parmesan cheese

Cut tomatoes in half. Combine garlic, tarragon, pepper, and cheese. Sprinkle over tomatoes; bake at 350°F/180°C until tender, about 30 minutes.

Recommended portion: ½ tomato (19 calories).

Florentine Tomatoes

Easy to do and delicious.

> 4 tomatoes
> 1½ pounds (675 g) fresh spinach, or 1 package frozen
> 1 tbsp. whipped margarine
> ⅛ tsp. nutmeg
> vegetable salt to taste
> black pepper to taste
> 2 tbsps. grated Parmesan cheese

Cut tomatoes in half. Bake in a lightly greased casserole for 10 minutes at 325°F/165°C. Heat spinach until leaves are wilted or ice is melted. Drain. Chop fine by hand or in blender; mix with margarine, nutmeg, salt, and pepper. Cook briefly until hot, pile on top of tomato halves, and sprinkle with cheese. Return to oven for 10 minutes.

Recommended portion: ½ tomato (68 calories).

Mushrooms Stuffed with Green Beans

FOR FOUR

Especially good with beef.

> ¼ cup grated Swiss cheese
> 1 cup (¼ L) steamed green beans, drained
> 1 tsp. minced onion
> vegetable salt to taste
> 12 medium-sized white mushrooms, caps only
> 2 tbsps. grated Parmesan cheese

Purée Swiss cheese, green beans, and onion in blender or food processor. Season. Pile into mushrooms and sprinkle with Parmesan. Bake in a shallow, lightly greased casserole at 375F°/190°C, for 12 to 15 minutes.

Recommended portion: 3 stuffed mushrooms (85 calories).

Variations: Use the same filling in artichoke bottoms. You may also substitute spinach or any other vegetable for the beans.

Artichoke Soufflé

FOR SIX

2 tbsps. whipped margarine
2 tbsps. flour
½ cup (1 dL) skim milk
1 tsp. grated onion
½ tsp. vegetable salt
4 egg yolks, beaten
2 cups (½ L) mashed, cooked artichoke bottoms
5 egg whites, beaten stiff

Melt margarine, stir in flour, and cook until bubbly. Add milk and cook until thick, stirring constantly. Add onion and seasoning, then yolks and artichokes. Cool slightly. Stir in ¼ of the stiffly beaten egg whites, then fold in the rest. Pour into lightly greased 1½-quart soufflé dish or ring mold. Set in pan of hot water. Bake at 350°F/180°C for 45 minutes. Let stand for 5 minutes if unmolding.

Recommended portion: ½ cup (90 calories).

Variations: Use sautéed, minced mushrooms, steamed mashed broccoli, or any other cooked or canned vegetable in place of artichoke.

Seafood

Seafood is much lower in calories than are animal meats. If you are not already a seafood fan, try to develop a taste for all kinds.

Poached Turbot

FOR FOUR

When buying turbot, be sure the flesh is firm and white.

1 cup (¼ L) dry white wine
2 cups (½ L) water
1 cup (¼ L) bottled clam juice
1 medium onion, sliced
1 medium carrot, sliced
a few sprigs of parsley
1 bay leaf
½ lemon, thin sliced
2 lbs. (900 g) turbot filets, skinned
vegetable salt to taste
1 tbsp. capers
4 slices lemon for garnish
parsley or watercress for garnish

Combine liquids, onion, carrot, parsley, bay leaf, and lemon in a saucepan. Bring to a boil, reduce heat, and simmer for 30 minutes. Strain. Cut turbot in 4 portions and arrange them in a lightly-foiled shallow casserole. Pour strained liquid over them. Cover and bake at 300°F/150°C for 20 minutes, or until fish flakes when tested with a fork. Remove filets to a warm platter. Return liquid to saucepan and reduce by half. Season, add capers, and pour over fish. Garnish with lemon slices and parsley or watercress.

Recommended portion: 1 8-ounce portion (400 calories).

Poached Salmon

FOR SIX

If you are lucky enough to have a fresh salmon, poach it by this simple recipe.

    enough water to cover salmon
    ½ cup (1 dL) vegetable salt
    1 lemon, sliced
    1 bay leaf
    1 3-pound (1350 g) fresh salmon
    lemon slices for garnish

Bring water, salt, lemon slices, and bay leaf to boil in a large pot or fish steamer. Put in the salmon. Simmer gently, covered, for 10 minutes. Remove the pot from the heat, leaving the lid on, and let the fish finish cooking in the warm liquid. When the water has come down to about the temperature of a hot broth (test it with your finger) lift out the fish. Now skin it carefully and serve with lemon slices.

It is important that the salmon be served warm, rather than hot from the boiling pot. There is nothing that dries out faster than steaming fish. If you worry about getting the fish out of the water whole and perfect, wrap the fish in a very large piece of cheesecloth before cooking, so that once it is done you can lift it out easily by holding on to the material at each end.

Recommended portion: ⅛ of fish (340 calories).

Trout with Red and Green Pepper Sauce

FOR FOUR

4 8-oz. (225 g) mountain or brook trout
1 tbsp. vegetable oil
4 stalks celery
4 slices onion
a few sprigs of parsley
4 carrots, thinly sliced
vegetable salt to taste
1 green pepper, seeded
1 sweet red pepper, seeded
2 tbsps. whipped margarine
1 bunch scallions
1 lemon, sliced thin

Clean, wash, and dry trout. Rub lightly with oil (if you like the flavor of olive oil, use it), and stuff with parsley and carrots. Put celery and onions on a baking tray covered with aluminum foil, and lay fish on top. Sprinkle lightly with vegetable salt. Bake uncovered at 350°F/180°C for 15–20 minutes. Run under broiler to crisp. Cut peppers in matchlike pieces. Drop in boiling water for 1 minute. Place fish on platter; remove vegetables. Cover with peppers and melted margarine. Decorate with scallion brushes and lemon slices.

Recommended portion: 1 trout (175 calories).

TO MAKE SCALLION BRUSHES:

Clean and trim scallions. Cut in 4-inch lengths. At each end of the scallion, with a very sharp knife, make several parallel 1-inch cuts, so that the onion looks like a double-ended paintbrush. Place in ice water — the cut ends will fan out. Do the same with other vegetables like celery, tiny squash, asparagus, carrot fingers.

Red Snapper with Grapefruit

FOR FOUR

4 4-oz. (115 g) red snapper filets
½ cup (1 dL) fresh or canned grapefruit juice
1 tbsp. whipped margarine, melted
vegetable salt to taste
paprika to taste
16 fresh grapefruit sections
2 tbsps. chopped parsley for garnish
4 slices lime or lemon for garnish

Marinate snapper in grapefruit juice for 2 minutes. Place in a lightly oiled, shallow casserole. Pour margarine over fish and sprinkle with vegetable salt and paprika. Bake at 300°F/

150°C until partially done, about 12 minutes. Top with grapefruit sections, 4 to each portion. Return to oven until fish flakes and grapefruit is hot. Run under broiler for 1 minute to color. Serve sprinkled with parsley and a twist of fresh lime or lemon.

Recommended portion: 1 4-ounce portion (254 calories).

Stuffed Flounder

FOR FOUR

4 oz. (120 g) shrimp, cooked and chopped
1 egg, slightly beaten
½ cup (1 dL) skim milk
1 tbsp. whipped margarine
½ cup (1 dL) mushrooms, chopped
1 tsp. chives, chopped
1 tsp. flour
1 1-lb. (450 g) flounder
2 tbsps. dry sherry
vegetable salt to taste
paprika to taste

Mix shrimp, egg, and ¼ cup of the milk. Melt margarine in small skillet. Sauté mushrooms and chives 1 minute. Add flour and cook until bubbly. Add shrimp mixture and cook until thickened. Split the flounder, separating top from bottom. Place bottom half in a lightly greased, shallow baking dish. Spread mixture over the fish, and top with the other half. Pour remaining milk and sherry over it. Sprinkle with seasonings. Bake at 300°F/149°C for 30 minutes, or until fish flakes.

Recommended portion: 4 ounces (304 calories).

Shrimp Creole

1 tbsp. whipped margarine
½ cup (1 dL) sliced onion
1 clove garlic, crushed
½ cup (1 dL) celery, sliced
¼ cup (½ dL) green pepper, sliced
2 cups (½ L) tomatoes, peeled and seeded
1 bay leaf
4 cloves
1 tsp. vegetable salt
24 medium shrimp, shelled
1 cup (¼ L) okra, steamed 4 minutes
¼ cup (½ dL) chopped parsley

Melt margarine and sauté onion, garlic, celery, and green pepper until soft, but do not brown. Add tomatoes, bay leaf, and cloves. Cook until thickened. Add shrimp. Cover and cook 3 minutes. Season. Serve over okra and sprinkle with chopped parsley.

Recommended portion: 6 shrimp with sauce and ¼ cup okra (100 calories).

Crabmeat Chantilly

FOR FOUR TO EIGHT

1 tbsp. whipped margarine
1 tbsp. shallots, minced
13 oz. (370 g) crabmeat, fresh or canned
2 tbsps. dry white wine
4 egg whites
1½ tbsps. Dijon mustard
¼ tsp. Worcestershire sauce
Parmesan cheese

Melt margarine, add shallots, sauté 1 minute. Add crabmeat and wine. Sauté until wine is evaporated, about 1 minute. Place in bottom of a lightly oiled, shallow, 1-quart casserole. Beat egg whites until almost stiff. Fold in mustard and Worcestershire sauce. Continue beating until stiff. Pile on top of crabmeat. Sprinkle lightly with grated Parmesan. Bake at 350°F/180°C until light brown.

Recommended portion: as appetizer, 3 ounces (72 calories); as entrée, 6 ounces (144 calories).

Poultry

POULTRY has fewer calories than meats and can be very interestingly prepared.

Rock Cornish Hens Parmesan

FOR FOUR

2 Rock Cornish hens
1 tsp. vegetable salt
2 tsps. whipped margarine
1 tbsp. shallots, finely diced
¼ cup (½ dL) finely chopped parsley
2 tbsps. Parmesan cheese, grated

Wash and dry hens and rub them with vegetable salt inside and out. Melt margarine in small saucepan. Add shallots and sauté 1 minute. Stir in parsley and cheese. Cool. Stuff in between skin and breast flesh of hens. Place in shallow casserole and bake uncovered at 450°F/230°C for 35 minutes or until done. Cut in halves or disjoint. Serve with pan juices.

Recommended portion: ½ hen with sauce (152 calories).

Chicken in Champagne

2 1½-lb. (675 g) broilers
1 tsp. vegetable salt
⅛ tsp. white pepper
⅜ cup (¾ dL) champagne
1 cup (¼ L) fresh mushrooms, sliced
½ cup (1 dL) chicken broth
2 tbsps. cognac

Wash and dry chickens and rub them with vegetable salt and white pepper. Lightly oil a roasting pan and roast the chickens at 450°F/230°C for 35 minutes or until done. Remove chickens from pan. Add champagne and mushrooms to drippings and sauté over high heat for 3 minutes. Add broth and simmer until juices are reduced by half. Disjoint chickens, pour mushrooms and juices over them. Ignite cognac and pour it over everything.

Recommended portion: ½ chicken (247 calories).

Ginger Roasted Chicken

FOR FOUR

2 1½-lb. (675 g) broilers
½ cup (1 dL) soy sauce
1 tbsp. gin
4 cloves garlic, crushed
1 tsp. honey
1 tbsp. fresh ginger root, shredded
8 small green onions, minced

Wash and dry chickens. Mix rest of ingredients and rub into chickens, inside and out. Let stand at least 1 hour. Place in a shallow pan and roast at 450°F/230°C for 35 minutes or until done, basting once with leftover marinade. Disjoint and serve with roasting juices.

Recommended portion: ½ chicken (275 calories).

Tandoori Roast Chicken

FOR FOUR

2 1½-lb. (675 g) broilers
3 cups (¾ L) low-calorie yogurt
6 cloves garlic, crushed
1½ tbsps. fresh ginger root, grated
¾ cup (1¾ dL) lime juice
2 tbsps. ground coriander seed
1 tbsp. ground cumin seed
2 tsps. cayenne pepper
1 tsp. powdered anise (optional)
1 lime, quartered, for garnish
thin slices of onion for garnish

Wash and dry chickens. Mix yogurt, garlic, ginger, lime juice, and spices. Rub chickens inside and out with mixture. Place in a bowl and cover with rest of mixture. Refrigerate for 24 to 36 hours. Turn once. Remove from marinade, place in a pan, and roast at 375°F/190°C until done (about 1½ hours), basting occasionally with marinade. Disjoint and serve with a wedge of lime and thinly sliced steamed onion ring.

Recommended portion: 3 ounces (165 calories).

Variation: Do turkey the same way.

Chicken with Chanterelles

FOR FOUR

Chanterelles are a variety of forest mushroom. Use fresh ones if you know how to handle them; or buy them canned, imported from France or Belgium, in gourmet food shops; or substitute fresh or canned mushrooms.

4 4-oz. (115 g) boned chicken breasts
¼ cup (½ dL) whipped margarine
1 clove garlic, whole
¼ tsp. paprika
¾ cup (1¾ dL) beef consommé
⅓ cup (¾ dL) cognac
10 oz. (285 g) chanterelles, washed and dried
vegetable salt to taste
2 tbsps. chopped parsley for garnish

Wash and dry chicken. Slice meat in 1-inch strips. Melt the margarine in a skillet. Add the garlic and paprika. Cook 1 minute, add chicken, and stir-fry for 3 minutes. Add consommé and deglaze pan. Heat cognac, ignite it, and pour it over the chicken; cover and simmer for 10 minutes. Remove chicken to serving platter. Add chanterelles or mushrooms to liquid left in skillet. Season. Heat thoroughly, remove garlic, and pour sauce over chicken. Sprinkle with chopped parsley.

Recommended portion: 4 ounces (188 calories).

Breast of Chicken Dublin Style

1 tsp. whipped margarine
¼ cup (½ dL) onion, thinly sliced
4 4-oz. (115 g) boneless chicken breasts
2 cups (½ L) chicken broth
1 cup (¼ L) Delicious apples, thinly sliced
vegetable salt to taste
2 tbsps. brandy

Melt margarine, add onion, sauté 1 minute. Add chicken breasts and cover with broth. Cover and simmer for 10 minutes. Add apples, cover, and cook until apples are soft, about 10 minutes. Season. Add brandy and ignite. Serve with apples and juices.

Recommended portion: 1 breast with apples and sauce (207 calories).

Fruited Breast of Chicken

FOR FOUR

4 6-oz. (170 g) boneless chicken breasts, flattened
vegetable salt to taste
1 tbsp. whipped margarine
1 banana
½ cup (1 dL) fresh or water-packed pineapple, diced
3 tbsps. lemon juice
3 tbsps. soy sauce
2 tbsps. chopped parsley for garnish

Wash and dry chicken breasts. Sprinkle lightly with vegetable salt. Melt margarine in a skillet. Slice banana on bias and brown the slices in the skillet. Remove the slices and keep warm. Add pineapple to the skillet and brown it. Add it to the banana and sprinkle with lemon juice. Broil chicken breasts, skin side down, for 5 minutes. Spoon half the soy sauce over them. Turn, broil 10 minutes, baste with rest of the sauce. Pour fruit over chicken and briefly place under broiler to heat. Sprinkle with parsley.

Recommended portion: 1 chicken breast, ¼ of fruit (219 calories).

Coq au Vin

FOR FOUR

1 tbsp. shallots
2 Rock Cornish hens, disjointed
4 small white onions
¾ cup (1¾ dL) beef consommé
¾ cup (1¾ dL) dry red wine
16 small whole mushrooms
vegetable salt to taste
fresh ground pepper to taste
2 tbsps. chopped parsley for garnish

Prepare skillet with nonstick vegetable spray or small amount of vegetable oil. Add shallots; sauté for 1 minute. Add hens, place under broiler until brown. Add onions, consommé, and red wine. Cover and simmer on top of stove for 30 minutes. Add mushrooms and cook uncovered over high heat, until liquid is reduced to one-quarter of its original volume. Season, sprinkle with parsley, and serve.

Recommended portion: ½ hen with 1 onion, 4 mushrooms (137 calories).

Breast of Chicken Piquante

4 6-oz. (170 g) boneless chicken breasts
1 tbsp. flour
½ tsp. vegetable salt
⅛ tsp. white pepper
1 tbsp. salad oil
1 tbsp. whipped margarine
½ tsp. shallots, minced
1 clove garlic, minced
juice of 2 lemons
¼ cup (6 cl) finely chopped parsley

Flatten chicken breasts. Lightly dust with mixture of flour, salt, and pepper. Shake off as much as possible. Heat oil and margarine; add shallots, garlic, and chicken. Sauté gently for 5 minutes. Turn once and cook 5 minutes more. Remove to platter. Add lemon juice to skillet and boil 1 minute. Correct seasonings, add parsley, pour over chicken, and serve at once.

Recommended portion: 1 chicken breast with 1 tablespoon sauce (203 calories).

Chicken Yakitori

FOR ONE

1 cup (¼ L) soy sauce
1 tsp. fresh ginger root, shredded
½ tsp. sugarless sweetener
½ cup (1 dL) dry white wine or sake
3½ oz. (100 g) boned chicken, cubed

Combine first four ingredients and cook over low heat for 15 minutes. Pour over chicken, which you have arranged on a skewer (I use bamboo). Broil for 2 minutes, turn, spoon the sauce over it, and broil 3 minutes more. Save the leftover sauce for future use.

Recommended portion: 3½ ounces plus 2 tablespoons sauce (183 calories).

Chicken Breast in Foil

FOR FOUR

1 tbsp. whipped margarine
1 tbsp. chopped green onions or shallots
4 4-oz. (115 g) chicken breasts
4 pieces of foil, 12" x 12"
8 canned or fresh mushrooms
½ cup (1 dL) dry white wine
a pinch of thyme or tarragon
vegetable salt to taste
chopped parsley to taste

Melt margarine in a skillet; add onions and chicken. Sauté 1 minute. Grease each piece of foil lightly with vegetable oil and place a chicken breast in the center. Add 2 mushrooms for each breast. Fold edges of foil upward to form individual cooking pans. Add wine to skillet and deglaze. Add seasonings. Pour liquid into each foil "pan." Fold edges together tightly. Bake at 350°F/180°C for 1 hour. Open when ready to eat, at the table. These are good for a box lunch or picnic, as they stay warm.

Recommended portion: 1 chicken breast plus sauce (205 calories).

Roast Turkey in White Wine

FOR TWELVE, WITH LEFTOVERS

1 14–16 lb. (7K) turkey
1 tbsp. tarragon
1 tbsp. vegetable salt
1 tbsp. paprika
1 medium onion, sliced
1 carrot, diced
1 stalk celery, diced
2 cloves garlic, crushed
2 cups (½ L) dry white wine

Wash and dry turkey. Rub with combined dry seasonings. Distribute vegetables in a roasting pan, place turkey on them, and roast uncovered in a 350°F/180°C oven for 3 hours. Baste occasionally with white wine. Spoon off as much fat as possible while cooking. Remove from oven and strain off all fat. Slice *thin*. Serve with unthickened pan juices.

Recommended portion: 3 ounces (162 calories).

This is the preparation we use for Thanksgiving dinner at The Greenhouse, and we get no complaints. We usually serve hot cranberries and Turnip Pudding (rutabagas) baked in an orange shell. You really will not miss the dressings and thickened giblet gravy you associate with Thanksgiving.

A pretty change for cranberries: Cranberry Sherbet served in a scooped-out red apple. Put in deep freeze for a couple of hours for a frosty look.

Oriental Chicken Salad

FOR ONE

This combination of the crisp cold lettuce and hot chicken is delightful to your taste buds.

1 cup (¼ L) finely shredded iceberg lettuce
1 4-oz. (115 g) chicken breast, or other parts, skinned and
   boned
½ cup (1 dL) soy sauce
1 tsp. whipped margarine
6 snow peas
½ scooped-out pineapple, chilled
1 tsp. grated orange peel

Shred lettuce (do not chop) and refrigerate. Cut chicken in strips. Dip chicken in soy sauce, or soy sauce diluted with water or dry white wine. Heat margarine until pan is hot. Add chicken and stir-fry for 1 minute. Add snow peas; cover and cook 1 minute more. Fill the pineapple cavity with the cold lettuce, add the chicken and whatever sauce clings to the chicken in cooking. Sprinkle with grated orange peel. Eat at once.

Total calories: 226.

Variations: Add hot bean sprouts, water chestnuts or mushrooms if you wish.

Squab in White Wine

FOR FOUR

4 12-oz. (340 g) squabs
2 tsps. vegetable salt
1 tbsp. shallots, minced
½ cup (1 dL) dry white wine
2 tbsps. chopped parsley

Wash and dry squabs. Place in a roasting pan. Sprinkle with vegetable salt and shallots. Roast at 425°F/220°C for 45 minutes, basting twice with wine. Remove squabs from pan. Add parsley to roasting juices along with any wine left over from basting. Simmer on top of stove for 1 minute and pour over squabs.

Recommended portion: 1 squab (165 calories).

Meat

IN CHOOSING MEAT recipes for you, I have not included much pork and beef because they are higher in fat content than veal and lamb. If you are steak-minded, limit your selection to lean cuts and your portion to 3 ounces uncooked weight or 2 ounces cooked.

The number of people each recipe serves will vary, depending on how many diners limit themselves to Greenhouse diet portions.

Veal Piccata

FOR FOUR

4 3-oz. (85 g) veal cutlets, thin
2 tbsps. whipped margarine
¼ cup (½ dL) dry vermouth or chicken broth
vegetable salt and pepper to taste
juice of one lemon
8 thin slices of lemon
2 tbsps. chopped parsley for garnish

Melt margarine in a skillet large enough to hold all the veal. Sauté veal over high heat for 2 minutes. Turn, and cook for another 2 minutes — no longer. Turn once more and immediately remove to serving dish and cover. Use vermouth or broth (or half broth, half vermouth) to deglaze the cooking pan. Season with salt and pepper and add lemon juice and slices. Bring to a boil and then pour over veal. Sprinkle with parsley.

Recommended portion: 3 ounces (203 calories).

Variations: Do the same with filet of sole or with thin slices of uncooked turkey or chicken.

Osso Buco

FOR FOUR

4 16-oz. (450 g) veal knuckles
1 tbsp. salad oil
½ cup (1 dL) diced onion
2 garlic cloves, sliced
4 ripe tomatoes, peeled and crushed
1 cup (¼ L) dry white wine
1 bay leaf
6 peppercorns
½ cup (1 dL) parsley, chopped
grated rind of 1 lemon
2 cups (½ L) chicken broth
vegetable salt to taste
4 lemon slices for garnish

Trim veal of any fat; there shouldn't be much. Heat oil in skillet and brown the knuckles. Add onion and garlic and cook until onion is soft. Add tomatoes, wine, seasonings, and broth. Cover and simmer until meat is tender and bone end is soft. Add more broth if necessary. When meat is tender, remove knuckles. Strain sauce, pushing as many of the cooked vegetables through the strainer as possible. Pour the strained sauce over the knuckles and let stand covered until ready to serve. Garnish with the lemon.

Recommended portion: 1 knuckle with sauce (210 calories).

Veal Loin Florentine

FOR FOUR

Make eyes at your butcher and have him or her bone a section of rack of veal and cut a pocket lengthwise in the meat. Remember — white or very pale pink veal is the best.

> 1 tbsp. whipped margarine
> 2 tbsps. minced shallots
> 1 cup (¼ L) mushrooms, sliced thin
> 1 lb. (450 g) fresh spinach, finely chopped
> 1 lb. (450 g) loin or boned rack of veal
> 1 tbsp. vegetable salt
> ½ cup (1 dL) beef broth
> ½ cup (1 dL) dry red wine or Madeira

Melt the margarine; add shallots, mushrooms, and spinach (no stems) and stir-fry 1 minute. Rub veal with vegetable salt. Stuff spinach mixture into pocket; tie firmly. Place in a roasting pan and roast uncovered at 450°F/230°C for 15 minutes. Reduce heat to 350°F/180°C and cook, basting twice with broth and wine, for about 40 minutes more, or until thermometer registers 170°F/77°C. Remove from the oven and cut off string. Strain the juices into saucepan and reduce them to half the original quantity. Slice the meat thinly and serve with the reduced juices.

Recommended portion: 3 ounces (208 calories).

Roast Veal with Oranges

FOR FOUR

1 lb. (450 g) boneless leg of veal
2 tsps. vegetable salt
1 tbsp. paprika
1 tbsp. grated orange peel
½ cup (1 dL) dry white wine
½ cup (1 dL) chicken broth
1 cup (¼ L) mandarin orange sections
slivered orange peel for garnish
chopped mint leaves for garnish

Rub veal with vegetable salt, paprika, and orange peel. Roast, uncovered, at 350°F/180°C for about 1½ hours, or until thermometer reads 170°F/77°C. Baste frequently with wine and broth. Add mandarin oranges during the last 15 minutes. Slice the meat thinly and serve with pan juices and oranges. Sprinkle with slivered orange peel and mint.

Recommended portion: 3 ounces (209 calories).

This is a good dinner for people who live alone. The left-over cold veal, sliced thin, is a good luncheon entrée, and cold veal diced into a jellied beef or chicken consommé makes a delightfully cool luncheon dish.

Roast Veal with Herbs

3 lbs. (1350 g) boneless leg of veal
1 tbsp. salad oil
1 tbsp. vegetable salt
½ tsp. dried tarragon
½ tsp. dried rosemary
½ tsp. oregano
1 tsp. paprika
2 tbsps. chopped parsley
2 tbsps. minced shallots
1 cup (¼ L) chicken broth
1 cup (¼ L) dry white wine
artichoke bottoms, canned (optional)

Remove any visible fat. Rub veal with salad oil. Mix dry ingredients with parsley and shallots and rub over the meat. Basting frequently with broth and wine, roast uncovered at 350°F/180°C for about half an hour, or until thermometer registers 170°F/77°C. Slice thin and serve with pan juices. If you wish, slice a few artichoke bottoms into the juices — so few calories you don't need to count them.

Recommended portion: 3 ounces (193 calories).

Lemon Roasted Lamb

FOR EIGHT TO TWELVE

6 lb. (2¾ K) leg or shoulder of lamb, trimmed
4 cloves garlic
1½ tsps. vegetable salt
½ tsp. white pepper
½ tsp. paprika
1 tbsp. fresh or dried mint leaves
2 tbsps. lemon juice

Cut 16 tiny pockets, 1 inch deep, all over the lamb. Cut garlic into fourths and stick one into each pocket. Mix remaining ingredients and rub over surface of lamb. Place fat-side-up on a rack in an open pan. Do not cover. Insert a meat thermometer in flesh, away from bone. Roast at 400°F/205°C for 15 minutes. Reduce heat to 350°F/180°C and cook for 1½ hours or until meat thermometer registers 170° for medium rare (best for flavor) or 180° for well done. Remove from oven and remove garlic. Let stand at least 10 minutes before carving. Slice thin; strain any fat from juices left in pan and serve. Good cold, too.

Recommended portion: 3 ounces of leg (159 calories); 3 ounces of shoulder (174 calories).

Veal Stew with Zucchini

FOR SIXTEEN

This is a pretty buffet dish — and the leftovers are delicious.

    4 lbs. (1800 g) lean veal, cut in 1 inch cubes
    ½ cup (1 dL) thinly sliced onion
    4 cups (1 L) chicken broth
    vegetable salt to taste
    1 tsp. grated lemon peel
    1 tbsp. slivered lemon peel, no white
    8 medium zucchini
    chopped parsley

Lightly brown veal and onion in a shallow pot. Add broth. Simmer until veal is tender, about 1 hour. Add seasoning and grated lemon peel. Let stand 1 hour. Quarter zucchini lengthwise. Reheat veal; add zucchini and slivered lemon peel. Cover and simmer 3 minutes. Sprinkle with parsley.

Recommended portion: 4 ounces plus 2 slices zucchini (210 calories).

Veal en Gelée

FOR FOUR TO SIX

1 lb. (450 g) veal stew meat, cut in fine dice
1¾ cups (4 dL) chicken broth
½ cup (1 dL) white wine
1 bay leaf
vegetable salt to taste
white pepper to taste
1 tbsp. gelatin
1 cup (¼ L) finely chopped parsley
1 scallion, chopped fine

Cover veal with water and cook until tender, about 1 hour. Heat chicken broth and wine with bay leaf for 30 minutes. Season. Add the gelatin, which has been softened in a little of the broth before it was heated. Divide in half and add veal to half of this mixture as it begins to thicken. Spread this in a shallow casserole. Add parsley and shallots to rest of gelatin mixture and pour over veal. Chill overnight in refrigerator.

Recommended portion: 4 ounces (280 calories).

Oriental Beef

FOR ONE

5 oz. (140 g) lean raw beef, thinly sliced
1 tbsp. dry sherry
2 tbsps. soy sauce
1 tsp. vegetable oil
½ clove garlic, crushed
¼ cup (½ dL) onion, thinly sliced
¼ cup (½ dL) celery, thinly sliced
3 mushrooms, thinly sliced
¼ cup (½ dL) green pepper, thinly sliced
¼ medium tomato, peeled and sliced lengthwise

Pour sherry and soy sauce over meat and marinate for about half an hour. If you do not like the flavor of soy, skip it and use 3 tablespoons sherry. Heat oil with garlic. Add onion and marinated beef. Stir rapidly for 30 seconds. Add remaining ingredients. Cover and cook 2 minutes. Serve at once.

Total calories: 195.

Variations: Any other vegetables could be used in place of those listed.

Filet of Beef with Lobster Tail

FOR EIGHT TO TWELVE

3 lbs. (1350 g) beef tenderloin
1 tsp. vegetable salt
½ cup (1 dL) soy sauce
2 tbsps. fresh ginger root, grated
½ cup (1 dL) onion, sliced
¼ cup (½ dL) dry sherry
3 lobster tails

Rub beef with vegetable salt, some of the soy sauce, and the ginger. Scatter onions in a shallow pan and place the beef on top. Roast in a 450°F/230°C oven for 30 minutes. Remove and let rest. Baste with half the sherry. Split lobster tails in half, loosen meat from shell. Rub lightly with soy sauce and bake in a 350°F/180°C oven for 15 minutes. Remove lobster from shell. Cut a pocket three quarters of the way through the roasted filet, from end to end, and stuff lobster into the cavity. Return to oven to heat, basting with rest of soy and sherry. Slice and serve with juices. The combination of flavors is delicious.

Recommended portion: 3 ounces beef plus 1 ounce lobster plus sauce (201 calories).

The easiest way to obtain twelve 3-ounce servings is to cut the filet in thirds, then cut each section in fourths.

You can use the leftover cooking juices to season vegetables, putting them once lightly through a sieve.

Marinated Flank Steak

FOR EIGHT TO TWELVE

1 2½–3 lb. (1¼ K) flank steak, lean
1 tbsp. salad oil
½ cup (1 dL) dry white wine
1 or 2 cloves garlic, minced
1 tbsp. onion, minced
a pinch of thyme
1 bay leaf
2 tbsps. chopped parsley or chives

Trim the steak of all visible fat. Place it in a shallow casserole. Mix and add the remaining ingredients. Cover and refrigerate overnight, turning it once. Remove the meat, reserving the marinade; place it on a flat pan and broil it 4 inches from the heat, 4 to 5 minutes. Turn it over and repeat on the other side. Slice thin diagonally and keep it warm while you make a sauce by deglazing the pan juices with the leftover marinade. Vary the flavor by using dry red wine in place of white, or by adding soy sauce, more garlic, and slivers of fresh ginger root.

Recommended portion: 3 oz. meat plus 1 tablespoon sauce (200 calories).

A 3-ounce portion, if cut properly, will yield 3 or 4 thin slices. I know that the amount of food we think we see affects our appetites. In fact, I sometimes cannot finish the 3 or 4 thin slices, whereas if the same 3 ounces are served as a solid piece of meat, I can quickly gobble it up and want more. Purely psychological!

Low-Calorie Desserts

DIETERS SOMETIMES ENDURE martyrdom because they think they cannot have desserts. Greenhouse guests look forward to their dessert at dinnertime, no matter how small it is. The American tradition of ending dinner with a sweet is hard to break, so why try? But keep to low-calorie desserts and fresh fruits.

Sherbets and Ices

There are many varieties of low-calorie sherbets and ices you can make at home using an ice cream maker — or simply in your own freezer.

Freezer-tray method: Put the prepared and mixed ingredients into a freezer tray or a mold and cover with foil. Freeze till the mixture becomes a thick slush, then stir or beat it to break up the larger crystals. Return tray to freezer. Repeat beating once or twice to give the sherbet the consistency of coarse, churn-frozen sherbet. Move trays to refrigerator some 20 minutes before serving.

Here's a tip: Use up low-calorie ice creams and sherbets

quickly. If you store them too long in the freezer, they become hard. If this happens, whip them briefly in a blender or
food processor before serving.

Cranberry Sherbet

ONE QUART

1 tbsp. gelatin
3 tbsps. lemon juice
3 cups (¾ L) unsweetened cranberry juice
2 cups (½ L) buttermilk
2 tsps. (or to taste) sugarless sweetener

Dissolve gelatin in lemon juice. Melt over hot water. Add to
remaining ingredients. Freeze in an ice cream maker or in a
tray in a regular freezer (p. 118). Nice with turkey or any
fowl.
Recommended portion: 4 ounces (44 calories).

Frozen Orange Bowl

ONE AND A HALF QUARTS

2 cups (½ L) fresh orange juice
½ cup (1 dL) lemon juice
4 cups (1 L) skim milk
2 tsps. sugarless sweetener
1 tbsp. grated orange peel

Mix all ingredients and freeze in an ice cream maker. Remove
and pack in a mold; cover and store in a freezer. Unmold and
serve with puréed strawberries or fresh raspberries.
Recommended portion: 1 thin slice, 2 ounces (22 calories).

Orange Ice

FOR EIGHT

3 cups (¾ L) orange juice
¼ cup (½ dL) lemon juice
1 cup (¼ L) water
2 tsps. sugarless sweetener
2 tbsps. grated orange peel

Mix all ingredients. Freeze in an ice cream maker or in a tray in your freezer (p. 118). Garnish with slivers of orange peel.
Recommended portion: 2 ounces (22 calories).

Pear Sherbet

FOR SIX

1 lb. (450 g) fresh pears, peeled and seeded; or use canned, water-packed pears
2 tbsps. lemon juice
1 cup (¼ L) water
1 tsp. sugarless sweetener
1 egg white, beaten to soft peaks

Cut pears in large dice and place in saucepan. Add lemon juice and water. Simmer for 10 minutes. Blend in food processor or blender. Add sugarless sweetener and egg white. Freeze in an ice cream maker or in a tray in your freezer (p. 118).
Recommended portion: 2 ounces (24 calories).

Watermelon Sherbet

FOR EIGHT

5 cups (1¼ L) watermelon meat
1 tsp. sugarless sweetener
2 tbsps. lemon juice
1 tsp. gelatin
a few grains of salt

Purée melon and sweetener in blender or food processor. Melt gelatin in lemon juice over hot water and add to purée along with the salt. Freeze in an ice cream maker or in a tray in the freezer (p. 180).

Recommended portion: 2 ounces (14 calories).

Variation: For fun, cut a cantaloupe or honeydew melon in half, scoop out the seeds, and fill the cavity with the ice. Cover each half with plastic wrap and return to freezer. When ready to serve cut each in fourths. Serve with fresh lime or lemon. (⅛ of a melon is 50 calories.)

Grape Ice

FOR SIX

3 cups (¾ L) unsweetened grape juice (any color)
3 tbsps. lemon juice
3 tbsps. sugarless sweetener

Mix all ingredients. Freeze in an iice cream maker or in a tray in your freezer (p. 180). Decorate with fresh mint leaves and a small bunch of fresh grapes.

Recommended portion: 2 ounces (14 calories).

Apple Sherbet

1 tbsp. gelatin
1 tbsp. cold water
2 cups (4⅔ dL) apple juice
2 egg whites, beaten stiff
4 apples (optional)

Dissolve gelatin in cold water. Heat 1 cup apple juice and add it to dissolved gelatin, then add 1 cup cold apple juice. Allow to begin to congeal, then fold in egg whites. Freeze in an ice cream maker until smooth. Pack into a scooped-out whole apple and freeze for an hour. Everything looks frosted.

Recommended portion: 2 ounces sherbet (32 calories); scooped-out apple with sherbet, if you eat the apple, is 72 calories.

Variation: Substitute cranberry juice for apple juice.

Strawberry Buttermilk Sherbet

FOR TWELVE

4 cups (1 L) buttermilk
¼ cup (½ dL) lemon juice
1 cup (¼ L) corn syrup
1 cup (¼ L) puréed strawberries
2 tsps. sugarless sweetener

Mix all ingredients and freeze in an ice cream maker or in trays in your freezer (p. 180). Serve a small scoop and place half a strawberry on top with a fresh mint leaf.

Recommended portion: 2 ounces, ¼ cup (58 calories).

Variation: Substitute any fresh fruit for the strawberries.

Vanilla Ice Cream

With the advent of the ice cream makers that you put in your freezer to do all the work, you can have homemade ice cream frequently.

1 tsp. gelatin
4 cups (1 L) skim milk
2 eggs
2 egg yolks
2 tsps. sugarless sweetener
1 tsp. vanilla
a pinch of salt

Dissolve gelatin in ¼ cup of the milk; scald the rest. Beat eggs and egg yolks and beat in the milk. Cook until thickened. Add gelatin. Cool. Add sweetener, vanilla, and salt. Freeze in an ice cream maker.

Recommended portion: 3 ounces (52 calories).

Variations:

Carob Ice Cream: Add ⅓ cup (¾ dL) carob powder.
Coffee Ice Cream: Dissolve 4 tablespoons instant coffee in the hot milk.
Eggnog Ice Cream: Ignite and add 2 tablespoons brandy or bourbon.
Grape Nut Ice Cream: Add ¼ cup (½ dL) Grape Nuts, and substitute almond extract for vanilla.
Mint Ice Cream: Substitute peppermint oil for vanilla, and tint with green or pink vegetable coloring.
Chocolate Ice Cream: Scald milk with 2 squares bitter chocolate, and increase sweetener if you wish. Taste!
Fruit Ice Cream: Add ½ cup (1 dL) puréed fresh fruit to partially frozen ice cream and continue freezing.

Low-Calorie Cheesecake

1 tbsp. gelatin
2 tbsps. lemon juice
½ cup (1 dL) skim milk, scalded
2 eggs, separated
2 tsps. sugarless sweetener
2½ cups (6 dL) ricotta cheese, low fat
1 cup (¼ L) crushed ice
1 tsp. grated orange peel

Dissolve gelatin in lemon juice; add hot milk. Put in blender. Add egg yolks, sweetener, and cheese. Whip at high speed for 2 minutes. Add crushed ice. Continue running at high speed until thoroughly blended. Beat egg whites until stiff. Add orange peel. Fold into the cheese mixture. Pour into an 8-inch spring-form mold. Chill until firm, about 24 hours. Serve with any kind of puréed fresh fruit.

Recommended portion: 4 ounces (67 calories) with 1 tablespoon puréed fresh fruit.

Soft Custard

FOR FOUR TO FIVE

2 egg yolks
2 cups (½ L) skim milk
1 egg white, beaten stiff
½ tsp. (or to taste) vanilla or lemon extract
sugarless sweetener to taste

Mix egg yolks and milk. Cook over low heat until thickened. Cool and flavor. Fold in the beaten egg white.

Recommended portion: ½ cup (62 calories).

Baked Custard

4 egg yolks
2 cups (½ L) skim milk
½ tsp. sugarless sweetener
1 tbsp. grated orange peel
½ tsp. vanilla

Beat egg yolks; add milk, sweetener, grated orange peel, and vanilla. Pour into individual baking cups, place in pan of hot water, and bake at 350°F/177°C until custard is set, about 50 minutes. You may sprinkle a few grains of nutmeg on each cup before baking. Serve with Orange Sauce (below). This is especially recommended as a dessert men will enjoy also.

Recommended portion: 1 cup and 1 tablespoon sauce (97 calories).

Variations: Add 1 tablespoon Grape Nuts to mixture; or add 1 tablespoon carob powder and leave out the orange peel.

Orange Sauce

½ cup (1 dL) fresh orange juice
½ cup (1 dL) water
1 tsp. sugarless sweetener
½ tsp. arrowroot
1 tbsp. slivered orange peel

Heat juice, water, sweetener, and arrowroot. Cool. Add peel.

Cold Lemon Soufflé

FOR FOUR TO SIX

1 tbsp. gelatin
¼ cup (½ dL) cold water
2 cups (½ L) skim milk
4 egg yolks
sugarless sweetener to taste
½ cup (1 dL) lemon juice
2 tbsps. grated lemon peel
8 egg whites, beaten stiff

Dissolve gelatin in cold water. Bring milk to a boil, add egg yolks, and beat. Cook until thick. Add gelatin. Cool. Add sweetener, lemon juice, and lemon peel. As mixture begins to congeal, fold in egg whites. Pile into a 2-quart soufflé dish and refrigerate.

Recommended portion: 1 cup (76 calories).

Variations: Use orange juice and orange peel, or lime juice and lime peel, instead of lemon.

Baked Apples

FOR FOUR

4 medium cooking apples — I like Rome Beauties
1 cup (¼ L) canned pear juice
½ cup (1 dL) water
½ tsp. cinnamon
4 slices lemon

Core apples and remove peel from the top half of each. Bring juice, water, cinnamon, and lemon to a boil; add apples and simmer until apples are just tender. Remove to a casserole. Boil liquid until it has been reduced by one half. Add sweetener if necessary. Pour over apples and bake at 350°F/180°C for 20 minutes. You may add a tablespoon or two of ignited cognac. Serve warm. Soft Custard is a nice sauce with the apples if you think you need one.

Recommended portion: 1 baked apple, 1 tablespoon sauce (119 calories).

Wine Jelly Parfait

FOR FOUR

1 tbsp. gelatin
1 tbsp. lemon juice
⅓ cup (¾ dL) orange juice
½ cup (1 dL) hot water
¾ cup (1¾ dL) orange juice
½ cup (1 dL) port
grated rind of orange
sugarless sweetener to taste

Sprinkle gelatin over first two juices and dissolve. Add hot water. Cool, then add orange juice, port wine, grated orange peel, and sweetener. Refrigerate until almost set, spoon into four parfait glasses, and decorate with fresh fruit if you like.

Recommended portion: ¼ recipe (75 calories).

Pears Poached in Red Wine

FOR FOUR

4 fresh pears, firm
2 cups (½ L) dry red wine
1 cup (¼ L) water
4 slices lemon
4 tsps. sugarless sweetener
½ tsp. cinnamon (optional)

Peel pears, leaving them whole. Drop into a pot with the wine, water, lemon, sweetener, and cinnamon. Cover and simmer for about 20 minutes or until pears are tender but not soft. Cool in syrup and chill. Serve as a dessert with a little of the syrup. You can also prepare these for breakfast, substituting water for the wine and serving them hot.

Recommended portion: 1 pear (87 calories).

Stewed Apples

FOR FOUR

4 Rome Beauty or Winesap apples
½ lemon, sliced thin
2 cups (½ L) water
1 tsp. sugarless sweetener

Peel and quarter apples. Add with peelings and lemon to water and sweetener. (The peelings give a pretty pink tinge to the fruit.) Simmer until tender. Cool; remove apples, strain sauce, and combine. Serve warm or cold.

Recommended portion: ¼ recipe (72 calories).

Variation: Add ½ cup canned mandarin orange sections.

Lemon Snow Pudding Ring

FOR EIGHT

2 tbsps. gelatin
¼ cup (½ dL) cold water
2½ cups (6 dL) boiling water
½ cup (1 dL) lemon juice
2 tsps. grated lemon peel
sugarless sweetener to taste
6 egg whites, beaten stiff

Dissolve gelatin in cold water. Add boiling water and stir until gelatin is completely·melted. Cool. Add lemon juice, grated lemon peel, and sweetener. When the mixture begins to thicken, fold in the egg whites. Pour into a 2-quart ring mold. Refrigerate until firm. Unmold and fill center with fresh fruit. You may add food coloring to the mixture if you are so inclined.

Recommended portion: 1 scant cup (24 calories).

Raspberry Sponge Pudding

FOR SIX

1 cup (¼ L) skim milk
4 egg yolks, beaten
½ tsp. vanilla
2 cups (½ L) fresh or frozen raspberries
sugarless sweetener to taste
4 egg whites, beaten stiff

Combine milk and egg yolks in top of a double boiler. Cook until custard is thick, stirring constantly. Remove. Add vanilla and cool. Rub berries through a sieve or put in blender.

Add to custard. Sweeten to your taste. Fold egg whites into custard. Serve in chilled, stemmed crystal for an elegant touch.

Recommended portion: 1 cup (93 calories).

Coffee Sponge

FOR FOUR

A favorite low-calorie dessert.

    1⅓ tbsps. gelatin
    1½ cups (3½ dL) cold coffee, brewed or made with
        instant coffee
    1 cup (¼ L) skim milk
    sugarless sweetener to taste
    3 egg yolks, beaten
    3 egg whites, beaten stiff

Dissolve gelatin in ¼ cup cold coffee. Heat milk; add the gelatin. Add the remaining coffee and sweeten to your taste. Add beaten egg yolks. Cool. As the mixture begins to congeal, fold in egg whites. Pile into individual crystal bowls.

Recommended portion: ½ cup (86 calories).

Old-Fashioned Prune Whip

FOR SIX

    1 cup (¼ L) puréed cooked prunes, or use prune baby
        food
    2 tbsps. lemon juice
    sugarless sweetener to taste
    5 egg whites, beaten stiff

Mix prunes and lemon juice. Sweeten. Fold egg whites into the prune mixture. Pile into a large crystal bowl and serve with Soft Custard.

Recommended portion: ¾ cup (65 calories).

Hot Apricot Whip

FOR SIX

1 cup (¼ L) dried apricots
2 slices lemon
1 tsp. sugarless sweetener
4 egg whites, beaten stiff

Place apricots in a saucepan and cover them with water. Add lemon and simmer until soft and water is absorbed. Purée in blender or food processor until smooth. Add sweetener. Cool. Stir ⅓ of beaten egg whites into apricot mixture; fold in the rest. Pile into a 1½-quart casserole, lightly greased. Bake at 350°F/180°C for 30 minutes, while you are eating your entrée. Serve at once.

Recommended portion: ⅙ recipe (81 calories).

PART IV

Greenhouse Indulgences
A Potpourri
This and That

Greenhouse Indulgences

NOT ALL THE GUESTS at The Greenhouse are on low-calorie diet regimes. We give already-slim guests the house diet of approximately 850 calories, and then add homemade rolls, muffins, and various desserts to bring the diet up to maintenance — and let each conscience be its guide.

English Custard

FOR TEN TO TWELVE

¾ cup (1¾ dL) sugar
3 cups (¾ L) milk
2 tbsps. butter
12 egg yolks, beaten until lemon yellow
1 tsp. vanilla
1 cup (¼ L) heavy cream (optional)

Scald sugar and milk together in double boiler. Add butter and egg yolks. Stir vigorously and cook until thickened. Remove from stove to cool. Add vanilla and cream, either whipped or unwhipped.

Crème Brulée

This is probably the most popular dessert at The Greenhouse.

2 cups (½ L) cream
4 egg yolks
2½ tbsps. granulated sugar
1 tsp. vanilla
¼ cup (½ dL) sifted light brown sugar

Heat cream in double boiler. Beat egg yolks, adding granulated sugar gradually. Remove cream from heat and pour over egg mixture very slowly, while stirring. Add vanilla. Pour into a 1½-quart casserole. Place in a pan of hot water and bake uncovered at 325°F/165°C for 45 to 50 minutes or until set. When custard is set, sprinkle with the sifted brown sugar. Place under broiler for a minute or so until sugar melts. Chill. This is a rich, smooth custard and should be served very cold.

Apple Pudding

FOR SIX

4 Delicious apples, peeled, cored, thinly sliced
½ cup (1 dL) butter
2 tbsps. white wine
1 cup (¼ L) dry white bread crumbs
a pinch of cinnamon
2 eggs
1 cup (¼ L) milk
2 tbsps. sugar
a pinch of salt

Sauté apples in butter and white wine until tender. Remove apples, add bread crumbs and cook until crisp. Spread crumbs in a buttered 1½-quart casserole. Cover with the apples. Sprinkle with cinnamon. Beat the eggs, milk, sugar, and salt together. Pour over the apples carefully, so as not to disturb crumbs. Bake at 325°F/165°C for 1½ hours. Serve warm with Grand Marnier Sauce.

Grand Marnier Sauce

1 cup (¼ L) whipping cream
½ cup (1 dL) sugar
3 tsps. lemon juice
6 tbsps. Grand Marnier
1 tsp. grated orange peel

Whip cream until soft peaks are formed. Fold in sugar and remaining ingredients. Spoon over pudding.

Quick Chocolate Mousse

FOR EIGHT

3 oz. (85 g) semisweet chocolate
1 oz. (30 g) bitter chocolate
¼ cup (½ dL) honey
1½ tsps. instant coffee
1½ tbsps. cognac
2 cups (½ L) whipping cream
1 cup (¼ L) additional whipping cream
semisweet chocolate, shaved, for garnish

Heat chocolates and honey in a double boiler until melted and smooth. Stir in coffee and cognac. Cool slightly. Whip the

2 cups of cream and fold in. Pour into 8 individual molds or a buttered 1-quart mold. Chill or freeze. At serving time, whip 1 cup cream and spread it over mousse. Sprinkle with chocolate.

Cold Chocolate Almond Soufflé

FOR EIGHT

1 tbsp. gelatin
¼ cup (½ dL) rum
4 oz. (115 g) semisweet chocolate
1 cup (¼ L) light cream
½ cup (1 dL) confectioners' sugar
½ tsp. salt
2½ cups (6 dL) heavy cream
¼ cup (½ dL) slivered almonds, toasted and salted
2 oz. (55 g) semisweet chocolate, shaved, for garnish
candied violets for garnish

Combine gelatin and rum in a cup and let stand 5 minutes. Put the cup in a pan of boiling water to melt the gelatin. Melt chocolate in cream; beat until smooth. Add gelatin, sugar, and salt. Let it cool until it begins to congeal. Beat heavy cream and set aside 1 cupful. Fold the rest into the chocolate mixture until smooth. Fold in almonds. Pour into buttered 1-quart soufflé dish. Refrigerate. Serve topped with remaining whipped cream and sprinkled with shaved chocolate and crushed candied violets.

Caramel Soufflé

FOR EIGHT

4 cups (1 L) granulated sugar
12 egg whites
butter for coating pan

Heat 1½ cups of the sugar in a skillet over medium heat until it becomes a brown syrup. Do not let it burn. Pour into a 3-quart soufflé dish or bundt pan, coating the sides and bottom. Cool. Rub the coated dish with butter. Beat egg whites until stiff. Gradually add 2 cups sugar to the egg whites, beating constantly. Melt the remaining sugar in a skillet, until it becomes syrup. Add 1 tablespoon water and cook until the syrup forms a thread. Pour into the egg whites, beating at medium speed on your mixer. Increase to high speed and beat for 12 minutes. Pour into the buttered dish. Place this in a pan of hot water and bake at 300°F/150°C for 1 hour or until firm but not browned. Turn out at once onto a serving tray.

If you wish to prepare the soufflé early in the day, leave it in the dish and, before serving, return it to a 350°F/180°C oven for about 20 minutes. It must be hot or warm to come out of the pan. Some of the caramel syrup will stay in the pan. Serve with English Custard.

Both the soufflé and the custard are so high in calories, they can well be classified as sinful. By the way, men adore this dessert.

Variation: I sometimes serve lightly broiled, sugared strawberries with this soufflé.

Cold Apricot Soufflé

2 lbs. (900 g) canned peeled apricots
4 eggs
3 egg yolks
⅛ tsp. salt
½ cup (1 dL) sugar
¼ cup (½ dL) cold water
2 tbsps. unflavored gelatin
¼ cup (½ dL) lemon juice
½ tsp. vanilla extract
¼ tsp. almond extract
2 tbsps. cognac
1 cup (¼ L) heavy cream

Drain the juice from the apricots and purée them in a blender or food processor. Set aside. In the food processor or with an electric mixer, beat the eggs, yolks, salt, and sugar at high speed until mixture is thick, about 15 minutes. Sprinkle the gelatin over the cold water and lemon juice in a cup. Let stand for a few minutes to soften and then place the cup in a shallow pan of hot water, over low heat, to dissolve the gelatin. Remove cup from hot water and set aside. When egg mixture has been sufficiently beaten, add vanilla and almond extracts, and cognac. Still beating at high speed, slowly add the dissolved gelatin. Reduce speed to low and mix in the puréed apricots. Remove from mixer. Whip the cream until it holds soft peaks. Fold 1 cup of the apricot mixture into the cream. Fold this mixture into the remaining apricot mixture. Pour into a buttered 2½-quart mold. Refrigerate for several hours. Unmold on a tray and surround with apricot preserves or fresh strawberries. Pour Apricot Sauce over top and sprinkle the fruit with shaved semisweet chocolate.

Apricot Sauce

1½ cups (3½ dL) apricot jam
½ cup (1 dL) water
2 tbsps. sugar

Combine ingredients, bring to a boil, and cook for 5 to 10 minutes, stirring constantly. Rub the sauce through a sieve. You may add 1 or 2 tablespoons kirsch, brandy, or any liqueur.

Souffléed Crepes

TWELVE MEDIUM OR SIXTEEN THIN CREPES

I find that my crepes are consistently more tender when I use cake flour, but there is no law that says you must. I use the same formula for dessert crepes, but I add more sugar.

CREPES:

1 cup (¼ L) sifted cake flour (spooned into measuring cup)
1–1½ cups (¼ L–3½ dL) milk, whole or skim
2 eggs, separated
¼ tsp. sugar
5 tbsps. butter or margarine, melted and cooled

Put flour in a bowl, add the milk and stir with a wire whisk until smooth. Add 2 egg yolks and 1 of the egg whites, un-beaten, and beat until well blended. Add sugar and butter. Let batter stand at least 1 hour. Fold in the remaining egg white beaten to soft-peak stage. Pour about 1 tablespoon butter into a hot crepe pan. Swish around until pan is completely coated. Pour off excess butter. Add about 1½ tablespoons of batter. Tilt pan until bottom is covered. Cook about half a minute, turn with a spatula, cook another half minute. Remove from pan and repeat process. You do not need to add more butter to pan. Pile crepes on top of one another; it is not necessary to put paper in between them.

If you prefer a thinner crepe, add the larger quantity of milk. If you're making them ahead of time, wrap them in clear plastic or foil. Crepes freeze satisfactorily. To use after freezing, defrost at room temperature — do not put in a hot oven or they will melt into one big glop. Regardless of what you put into a crepe, the important thing to remember is to roll it loosely — both the crepe and the filling retain their flavor and texture better this way.

FILLING:

2 eggs, separated
½ cup (1 dL) sifted all-purpose flour (spooned into cup)
½ cup (1 dL) sugar
1 tbsp. Grand Marnier
a pinch of salt
a drop of vanilla
1 cup (¼ L) milk, scalded
powdered sugar

Mix egg yolks and flour. Add sugar, Grand Marnier, salt, and vanilla. Mix thoroughly. Gradually add the milk, stirring constantly to avoid lumping. Cook over medium heat until mixture thickens. Cool but don't chill. Fold in stiffly beaten egg whites. Spread a little over each crepe, fold into a pillow shape. Place in lightly buttered casserole and sprinkle with powdered sugar. Reheat for 5 minutes in a 500°F/260°C oven. Serve at once — with Apricot Sauce.

Netta Blanchard's Irish Chocolate Cake

Netta Blanchard is a lovely Irish lady straight from Dublin. This was her mother's recipe, made with Irish Coffee Liqueur. This liqueur is sometimes difficult to find, so I substitute Kahlua. When Neiman-Marcus had its Irish Fortnight I had this cake served at the opening ball. It met with raves and still does every time it is served. The sauces with it were my addition. Being allergic to alcohol, I sometimes serve the cake with ice cream and hot fudge sauce instead — and it is almost as welcome. Not quite!

¾ cup (1¾ dL) butter, softened
2 cups (½ L) sugar
¾ cup (1¾ dL) cocoa, sifted
4 eggs, separated
1 tsp. baking soda
2 tbsps. cold water
½ cup (1 dL) cold coffee
½ cup (1 dL) Irish Coffee Liqueur
1¾ cups (4 dL) thrice sifted cake flour (spooned into
    measuring cup)
2 tsps. vanilla

Cream butter and sugar. Add cocoa and beat in egg yolks, one at a time. Dissolve baking soda in water, and combine with coffee and liqueur. Add to the batter alternately with the flour. Add vanilla. Fold in stiffly beaten egg whites. Turn into a greased and lightly floured 9-inch bundt pan. Cook in moderate oven 325°F/165°C for 45 minutes.

GLAZE:

1 cup (¼ L) Irish Coffee Liqueur
1 cup (¼ L) powdered sugar

Turn cake out onto a plate while still warm and prick or pierce all over with a skewer. Combine liqueur and sugar and spoon this glaze mixture all over cake until it is completely soaked. Cover with foil and store in refrigerator.

I fill the center with Grand Marnier Sauce. To serve the cake, I slice it, cover each slice with this sauce, and then add a good serving of Apricot Sauce.

Cheddar Cheese Apple Pie

3 lbs. (1350 g) greening apples
1 cup (¼ L) sugar
2 tbsps. flour
½ tsp. cinnamon
1 tsp. lemon peel
⅛ tsp. salt
an unbaked 9″ pie shell
½ cup (1 dL) flour
¼ cup (½ dL) sugar
½ cup (1 dL) cheddar cheese, grated
¼ cup (½ dL) melted butter

Peel and core the apples and slice them thinly. Combine the next five ingredients, add the apples, and arrange this mixture in the pie shell. Combine the remaining ingredients and sprinkle them over the apples. Bake at 400°F/205°C for 40 minutes or until apples are tender. Serve warm with sour cream spread over the top.

Hot Fruit Curaçao

1 29-oz. (820 g) can freestone peaches, drained (reserve syrup)
1 30-oz. (850 g) can whole apricots, seeded and drained
2 bananas, freshly sliced
3 oranges, peeled and sectioned
juice of one lemon
grated rind of one orange plus 2 tbsps. slivered rind
¼ cup (½ dL) curaçao

Place fruit in shallow baking dish. Mix lemon juice with peach syrup and pour over fruit. Add orange rinds. Bake at 350°F/180°C for 25 minutes. Cool slightly, then pour curaçao over. Serve warm or hot, with or without whipped cream. Do not reheat after adding liqueur.

Strawberries Excellent

FOR SIX

2½ qts. (2½ L) strawberries
6 tbsps. brandy
7 tbsps. curaçao
1 cup (¼ L) whipping cream
1 pt. (½ L) pineapple ice or sherbet

Wash and hull 2 quarts (2 L) of the strawberries. Place them in a serving bowl (crystal is prettiest). Cover with the brandy and 6 tablespoons of the curaçao. Let stand in refrigerator for several hours. Whip the cream. Purée the remaining berries in a blender. Fold the purée into the whipped cream and add the tablespoon of curaçao. Just before serving put six scoops of pineapple ice or sherbet on top of the berries. Cover with the whipped cream mixture.

Pineapple Ice with Peaches

FOR EIGHT

This is a pretty dessert to bring to the table. It's good too in place of a more elaborate birthday cake: you can stick long Danish tapers into the ice, light them and present it. Spectacular!

3 pts. (1½ L) pineapple ice or sherbet
2 lbs. (900 g) canned peaches (white ones are
   especially pretty)
1 tsp. vanilla
26 oz. (735 g) frozen raspberries, thawed
¼ cup (½ dL) kirsch
½ cup (1 dL) sliced blanched almonds, lightly toasted

Pack ice into a ring-shaped mold and return it to the freezer. Drain peaches, reserving syrup. Reduce the syrup by one half over high heat. Cool. Purée berries in blender. Strain. Combine reduced syrup, berry purée, kirsch, and vanilla. Pour over peaches and chill. Just before serving, unmold the ice and arrange the peaches in the center or around it. Pour the raspberry sauce over everything and sprinkle with nuts.

Irish Tea Scones

ONE DOZEN LARGE SCONES

2 cups (½ L) all-purpose flour
2½ tbsps. sugar
salt to taste
2½ tbsps. baking powder
¾ cup (1¾ dL) butter, softened
2 eggs, beaten
milk to bind

Sift flour, sugar, salt, and baking powder together. Stir into the butter, along with the eggs. Add just enough milk to bind ingredients together. Turn out on a floured board; roll out to about ½-inch thick. Cut into diamonds, triangles, or rounds and bake at 350°F/180°C for 25 minutes.

Orange Muffins

THREE DOZEN SMALL MUFFINS

These make a good picnic dessert too.

> 1 cup (¼ L) butter or margarine
> 1 cup (¼ L) sugar
> 2 eggs
> 1 cup (¼ L) buttermilk
> 1 tsp. baking soda
> 2 cups (½ L) all-purpose flour, sifted
> grated rind of 2 oranges
> ½ cup (1 dL) golden raisins
> juice of 2 oranges
> 1 cup (¼ L) brown sugar

Cream butter and sugar, add eggs, beat till well mixed. Dissolve the baking soda in the buttermilk, and add it, alternately with the flour, to the egg mixture. Add orange rind and raisins. Fill well-buttered muffin pans two-thirds full and bake at 400°F/205°C for 20 or 25 minutes. Mix orange juice with brown sugar. Spoon over muffins and remove them from pans immediately.

Variation: Use pecans in place of the raisins. I like to make small muffins and freeze them and eat them frozen. They taste like candy.

Refrigerator Bran Muffins

EIGHT DOZEN

You can store this batter in four covered quart jars in the refrigerator. It keeps perfectly for as long as two months.

5 cups (1¼ L) All-Bran cereal
2½ cups (6 dL) raisins
2 cups (½ L) boiling water
1 cup (¼ L) white sugar
1 cup (¼ L) corn oil
2 cups (½ L) molasses
4 eggs, well beaten
1 qt. (1 L) buttermilk
5 cups (1¼ L) flour
5 tsps. baking soda
1 tsp. salt

Combine 2 cups of the cereal and all the raisins. Pour boiling water over them and set aside to cool. In a very large bowl combine sugar and oil. Stir in, one at a time, the molasses, eggs, buttermilk, and remaining cereal. Mix together the flour, baking soda, and salt and add this to the batter. Lastly, add the cooled raisin-bran mixture. The batter is now ready to use; or you can refrigerate it for future use. To bake muffins, spoon batter into buttered muffin pans (filling each section about two-thirds full) and bake at 400°F/205°C for exactly 20 minutes. Allow to cool slightly in pans, on a rack — the muffins come out of the pans more easily if given a short rest period.

A Potpourri

IN THIS SECTION I'd like to share with you some of my old favorites and new flights of fancy. They should appeal to the non-dieting members of your family, and to you when you're not thinking about the bathroom scales.

Gazpacho Blanco

FOR TWELVE

3 small cucumbers, peeled and diced
1 clove garlic, crushed
3 cups (¾ L) chicken broth
2 cups (½ L) sour cream
1 cup (¼ L) plain yogurt
3 tbsps. white vinegar
salt and pepper to taste
4 medium tomatoes, peeled and diced
½ cup (1 dL) diced green onions (white part only)
½ cup (1 dL) chopped parsley
4 oz. (115 g) slivered toasted almonds

Purée cucumbers, garlic, and 1 cup of the chicken broth in blender. Add remaining broth, sour cream, yogurt, vinegar, salt, and pepper. Mix thoroughly and chill. Present it in a chilled bowl, with the tomatoes, onions, parsley, and almonds served separately in small bowls or demitasse cups.

Gin Soup

FOR SIX TO EIGHT

Here's a different twist in the soup department — especially good on a cold day.

    2 tbsps. butter
    2 tbsps. finely diced onion
    2 tbsps. finely diced celery
    2 cups (½ L) canned clam juice
    2 cups (½ L) canned chicken broth
    2 cups (½ L) whipping cream
    2 tbsps. cornstarch
    ⅔ cup (1½ dL) gin
    1 tsp. dill weed
    2 tbsps. chopped chives
    2 tbsps. chopped parsley
    salt and pepper to taste

Melt butter in large saucepan. Add onion and celery, and sauté for 1 minute. Add clam juice, broth, and cream. Bring to a boil. Mix cornstarch with the gin and add. Bring to a boil again. Reduce heat; simmer for 10 minutes. Add dill, chives, and parsley, and season to your taste.

Garden Salad

1 head red lettuce
1 head romaine
1 cup (¼ L) cauliflower flowerets
1 cup (¼ L) zucchini, sliced
1 cup (¼ L) yellow squash, sliced
1 small cucumber, sliced
¼ cup (½ dL) slivered green onion
2 medium potatoes, cooked, peeled, thinly sliced
1 cup (¼ L) slivered celery, blanched
½ cup (1 dL) slivered green pepper, blanched
¾ cup (1¾ dL) Green Herb Dressing
2 hard-cooked eggs, chopped
a few pickled beets
1 bunch watercress
chopped parsley or chives for garnish

Make a bed of the lettuce leaves on a large platter. Arrange vegetables on top, as you see fit. Cover with Green Herb Dressing (or serve the dressing on the side). Garnish with chopped eggs, beets, watercress, and parsley or chives.

Cobb Salad

FOR EIGHT

1 head romaine, finely chopped
8 slices crisp bacon, crumbled
4 oz. (115 g) Roquefort cheese, broken into bits
3 tomatoes, peeled, seeded, and finely diced
2 avocados, peeled, seeded, and finely diced
2 hard-boiled eggs, finely chopped
4 strips pimiento

Put romaine in bowl. Arrange remaining ingredients in decorative sections on the lettuce, like wedges of a pie. Refrigerate. Serve with Pear Vinegar Dressing.

Green Chile Salad

FOR EIGHT

¾ cup (1¾ dL) salad oil
½ cup (1 dL) white vinegar
2 tbsps. sugar
1 clove garlic, minced
a pinch of white pepper
¼ tsp. salt
¼ cup (½ dL) slivered celery
2 tbsps. sliced green onion
½ cup (1 dL) tomatoes, peeled, seeded, diced
2 oz. (55 g) green chiles, diced
1¼ lbs. (565 g) fresh spinach, washed and trimmed
4 tomatoes, peeled and halved
chopped parsley for garnish

Mix first ten ingredients and refrigerate for several hours. Arrange spinach leaves on shallow tray or in bowl. Add tomatoes. Pour the chile sauce over and chill. Sprinkle with chopped parsley when ready to serve.

Asparagus Salad

1 head red lettuce or watercress
1 ripe avocado
1 tbsp. lemon juice
8 stalks asparagus, cooked and chilled
1 tbsp. capers
4 slices bacon, cooked crisp and crumbled
2 tbsps. additional lemon juice
⅓ cup (¾ dL) salad oil
salt and pepper to taste

Make a bed of the lettuce leaves or watercress in a bowl or on a tray. Peel avocado, halve it lengthwise, remove seed, and slice thinly lengthwise. Sprinkle with fresh lemon juice. Arrange avocado and asparagus on the lettuce and sprinkle with capers and bacon. Mix lemon juice and salad oil, season to your taste, and sprinkle over lightly. Will keep in refrigerator for a few hours.

Fennel Salad

FOR FOUR

This is my favorite salad.

2 medium-sized bulbs of fennel
4 tbsps. salad oil
2 tbsps. wine vinegar
whites of 2 hard-cooked eggs, chopped fine
2 tbsps. capers
2 tbsps. chopped parsley

Place fennel in ice water for one hour. Remove, dry, and slice very thin. Mix oil, vinegar, egg whites, capers, and parsley. Pour over fennel and toss.

Spinach and Jerusalem Artichoke Salad with Creamy Italian Dressing

FOR EIGHT

With hot French bread, good cheese, and red wine, this would be a great supper.

1 cup (¼ L) olive oil
⅓ cup (¾ dL) red wine vinegar
¼ cup (½ dL) sour cream
½ tsp. dry mustard
2 tbsps. sugar
¼ cup (½ dL) chopped parsley
2 cloves garlic, minced
1½ tsps. salt
1¼ lbs. (565 g) fresh spinach
4 oz. (115 g) Jerusalem artichokes, sliced
8 slices crisp bacon, diced

Mix the oil, vinegar, sour cream, mustard, sugar, parsley, garlic, and salt. Wash and trim spinach and place in large salad bowl. Add the artichokes and bacon and toss with enough dressing to coat. You may also add sliced or diced pickled beets, about 4 each, or avocado.

The dressing will not keep, so be sure to use it up.

Variations: Add hard-cooked egg (sliced); cherry tomatoes (halved); pickled beets (sliced or diced); or avocado.

[154]

Fettucine Alfredo

FOR EIGHT

Soothing! I call it mama food.

> 1 lb. (450 g) fettucine
> 1 cup (¼ L) butter, softened
> 1 cup (¼ L) cream at room temperature
> 2 cups (½ L) grated or shredded Parmesan cheese

Cook pasta in 8 quarts of boiling water to which 2 table-spoons salt have been added, about 8 minutes or until *al dente*. Drain pasta, but do not rinse, and immediately pour it onto a heated platter or into a heated bowl. Toss with butter, cream, and cheese until the cheese and butter are completely melted. Serve at once.

Teased Eggs

FOR EIGHT

One of our guests sent me this recipe.

> 8 hard-cooked eggs
> 3 tbsps. butter or margarine
> 3 tbsps. flour
> 2 cups (½ L) milk
> 1 cup (¼ L) sour cream
> 1 tbsp. grated onion
> 1½ tbsps. horseradish
> a few drops hot pepper sauce
> salt and pepper to taste
> 1 lb. (450 g) cooked shrimp, chopped fine, or shredded
>   crabmeat
> ½ cup (1 dL) Parmesan or grated Swiss cheese

Halve the eggs and mash the yolks. Melt the butter, add flour, and cook 1 minute. Add milk and cook over medium high heat, stirring, until thickened. Add sour cream and seasonings. Combine half a cup of this sauce with the seafood and the mashed yolks, and stuff it into the whites. Arrange them in a buttered, shallow casserole, stuffed side up. Pour the remaining sauce over them and sprinkle them with cheese. Bake at 300°F/150°C until hot and bubbly, about 30 minutes. Serve with link sausage, hot biscuits, and hot broiled fruit. You can substitute cooked chicken or ham for the seafood. I find it a most satisfactory brunch dish.

Cream Cheese Soufflé

FOR EIGHT

A fine and unusual accompaniment to a main course.

> 4 eggs, separated
> a pinch of salt
> 1 tsp. flour
> ¼ tsp. dry mustard
> a pinch of cayenne pepper
> ¾ cup (1 ¾ dL) cream cheese, softened to room
>   temperature
> 1 cup (¼ L) sour cream

In a big bowl, beat yolks of eggs until light and creamy. Add salt, flour, mustard, and cayenne. Blend cream cheese and sour cream until smooth. Add to egg yolks and beat with electric beater until smooth. Beat egg whites until stiff but not dry, and fold into yolk mixture. Transfer to ungreased 1½-quart soufflé dish. Place dish in pan of water and bake at 300°F/ 149°C for 1 hour.

Variation: Substitute 1 teaspoon sugar for the mustard and pepper, and serve it hot as a dessert — with puréed fresh strawberries or raspberries (strain to get rid of the raspberry seeds!).

Eggplant and Mushroom Casserole

FOR EIGHT

3 medium eggplants, peeled
1 cup (¼ L) finely chopped onion
8 tbsps. butter
4 eggs, beaten
1 cup (¼ L) mayonnaise
1 lb. (450 g) finely chopped fresh mushrooms
salt and pepper to taste
9 tbsps. cream cheese, softened
¼ cup (½ dL) finely chopped parsley
a pinch of thyme
3 tbsps. grated Gruyère cheese
¼ cup (½ dL) fine white bread crumbs

Cover eggplants with water and 1 tablespoon salt, and let stand for 30 minutes. Drain and cook in fresh water until tender. Drain well. Cut in cubes and place in large bowl. Sauté the onion in 2 tablespoons butter, until yellow. Add to eggplant. Stir in eggs and mayonnaise. Sauté mushrooms in 4 tablespoons butter. Add to the eggplant mixture. Mix thoroughly. Season to taste. Place in a buttered 2-quart casserole. Mix cream cheese with parsley, thyme, Gruyère, and bread crumbs. Spread over top of casserole mixture. Sprinkle with 2 tablespoons melted butter. Bake at 350°F/180°C until set and browned, about 40 minutes. You can make this ahead of time and refrigerate it until you're ready to bake and serve it.

Peas in Sour Cream

FOR EIGHT

A great company dish.

> 20 oz. (565 g) frozen or fresh peas
> 1 cup (¼ L) sour cream
> 1 tsp. horseradish
> 1 tsp. chopped fresh mint
> 1 tsp. Pernod (optional)
> 2 tbsps. thinly sliced scallions
> 1 apple, unpeeled, finely diced
> salt to taste

Thaw peas if frozen; cook until just tender, if fresh. In a large bowl, mix sour cream, horseradish, mint, Pernod, and scallions. Add peas and apples. Season with salt. Chill. Serve as a salad or a cold vegetable.

Scalloped Onions and Peanuts

FOR SIX

> 12 small white onions
> 1 cup (¼ L) diced celery
> 4 tbsps. butter
> 3 tbsps. flour
> 1 tsp. salt
> ⅛ tsp. pepper
> 1 cup (¼ L) milk
> ½ cup (1 dL) light cream
> ½ cup (1 dL) Spanish peanuts
> paprika for garnish

Wash and peel onions and cook in boiling salted water until tender. Drain. Prepare the celery the same way. Make a cream sauce: melt butter in saucepan, add flour, salt, and pepper; cook over low heat until bubbly; add milk and cream and cook until thick. In a buttered casserole, layer the onions, celery, and peanuts. Cover with the cream sauce, sprinkle with paprika, and bake at 350°F/180°C until bubbly and brown.

Zucchini Collage

FOR SIX

1 lb. (450 g) zucchini
¼ cup (½ dL) butter
¼ cup (½ dL) finely diced onion
½ clove garlic, finely diced
½ cup (1 dL) cherry tomatoes, halved (or one small tomato sliced thin)
salt and pepper to taste
2 tbsps. toasted sesame seeds
¼ cup (½ dL) finely chopped parsley

Wash zucchini and slice diagonally. Blanch 1 minute. Drain. Melt butter, add onion and garlic, sauté until soft and golden. Add zucchini; cover, and cook 2 minutes. Add tomatoes; cover, and cook 1 minute. Season with salt and pepper. Toss with sesame seeds and parsley.

Rice with Pine Nuts

¼ cup (½ dL) butter
2 tbsps. minced onion
1 cup (¼ L) rice
2½ cups (6 dL) consommé (beef or chicken)
4 oz. (115 g) pine nuts, toasted
¼ cup (½ dL) chopped parsley

Melt butter, add onion, sauté 1 minute. Add rice and con-sommé. Cover, bake at 350°F/177°C for 45 minutes. Stir in pine nuts and parsley. Correct seasonings.

Wild Rice and Apples

¾ cup (1¾ dL) wild rice
1½ cups (3½ dL) hot consommé
¾ cup (1¾ dL) white wine
2 Delicious apples, peeled and sliced thin
3 tbsps. butter
1 tbsp. brandy

Put rice, consommé, and wine in a buttered casserole. Cover and bake at 400°F/204°C for 1 hour or until rice is tender. Sauté apples in butter until tender. With a fork stir the apples into the rice; ignite brandy, add it, and serve.

Greenhouse Frankfurters

FOR EIGHT

¼ cup (½ dL) raisins
¼ cup (½ dL) cold water
8 all-beef frankfurters
½ cup (1 dL) dry white wine
½ cup (1 dL) plain yogurt
1 ½ tbsps. Dijon mustard

Cover raisins with water and let stand until plump. Put the frankfurters in a skillet with the wine and raisins. Cover and cook 5 minutes. Uncover, and let the wine reduce by half, then stir in the yogurt mixed with mustard. Heat, and then serve at once. Good with Jerusalem artichokes.

Sautéed Beef with Leeks and Mushrooms

FOR FOUR

¾ oz. (20 g) dried Chinese mushrooms
4 tbsps. peanut oil
1 cup (¼ L) leeks, white part only, thinly sliced
    diagonally
1 lb. (450 g) beef tenderloin, sirloin, or flank, sliced thin
1 tbsp. soy sauce
1 tsp. cornstarch
¼ cup (½ dL) water
a few drops sesame oil
1 tbsp. sherry

Soak the mushrooms in cold water for ½ hour. Drain, trim, and slice them. Preheat skillet or wok to a very high temperature. Swirl 2 tablespoons of oil into skillet and add leeks and dried mushrooms. Cook 1 minute, stirring constantly. Remove from skillet and keep warm. Rub skillet with paper towels, being careful not to burn your fingers. Add remaining 2 tablespoons oil and the sliced beef. Cook 2 minutes, stirring constantly. Add the cooked vegetables and the soy sauce and cook 1 minute more. Mix cornstarch with water and add to skillet. Cook 1 minute. Add sesame oil and sherry just before removing from heat.

Crown Roast of Lamb

FOR SIX

a 16-rib crown roast of lamb, well tied
salt and pepper to taste
rosemary or oregano to taste (optional)
1 clove garlic, slivered
1 cup (¼ L) beef consommé
1 tbsp. currant jelly
1 tbsp. red wine vinegar

Sprinkle lamb with salt and pepper (and herbs, if you like), inside and out. Make small cuts in the roast and insert garlic. Place an empty can or ovenproof bowl in center to hold crown in shape. Cover ends of chops with foil. Roast at 400°F/205°C for 20 minutes. Reduce to 350°F/180°C and roast for 40 minutes, or until internal temperature is 140°F. Remove meat from roasting pan and deglaze pan with beef consommé. Add jelly and vinegar. Cook until jelly is melted, and serve in a gravy boat.

Fill the center of the roast with vegetables. I like sautéed mushrooms and little white onions, or mushroom soufflé. For low-calorie preparation, skip the jelly.

This and That

The Mexicans have a *dicho* all Americans should adopt: *Salud, amor, pesetas, y tiempo para gozarlos;* which means, "Health, love, wealth, and time to enjoy them." I would add another: Eat with pleasure and moderation in all things.

❧

A lovely party bread, high in calories, is French bread sliced thick, diagonally, spread with a mix of butter, Port Salut cheese, and a whiff of garlic, and then toasted.

❧

Yuan Mei, a Chinese scholar, wrote, "Into no department of life should indifference be allowed to creep, into none less than into the domain of cookery." He must have been thinking of vegetable cookery. Surely mediocrity has no business in their consideration and preparation.

❧

Let's appreciate the green chile more. It adds spice to meat, sandwiches — just about everything. This concoction will keep for several days:

3 7-oz. (200-g) cans whole green chiles
1 cup (¼ L) white vinegar
1 cup (¼ L) sugar
1 tsp. dill seeds
1 tsp. salt

Cut chiles into bite-size pieces. Leave all seeds in. Mix sugar, vinegar, dill, and salt, until sugar is dissolved. Refrigerate at least 24 hours before serving. I add strips of red sweet pepper when it's in season.

❧

Serve lamb either hot or cold — not lukewarm.

❧

Seafood of any kind is better fresh than frozen. But when fresh seafood is unavailable, don't ignore the individual servings of frozen fish carried by most markets today. I find defrosting before cooking does improve the flavor, and defrosting in skim milk is still better.

❧

Marinated peppers make a delightful salad to serve with fish, Seed and freeze red peppers when they appear in the markets, for they are not available year-round. Substiute canned green chiles for a more piquant flavor.

❧

For added dash, sprinkle a few gratings of the peel of any citrus fruit over servings of vegetables, salads, fruits. Grate several oranges at a time, and freeze the gratings to have them readily available.

While traveling in Italy, I was impressed with the custom of serving fruit on a bed of ice. I have adopted the idea when dieting, and it's a very pretty practice any time. The fruit is cold and delicious, and looks like so much more.

❧

A quick but unusually good tidbit for people who like to munch with their cocktail:

GERTIE COTTLE'S CRISPS

2 heaping tsps. powdered cardamom
¾ stick butter or margarine
1 package flour tortillas

Mix cardamom and butter and spread completely over the tortillas. Bake in a shallow pan, at 250°F/120°C for 45 minutes to 1 hour, until crisp. Cool and break into irregular pieces. Vary by using cinnamon instead of cardamom.

❧

If you like to serve crepes with a filling, the important thing to remember is to roll each crepe loosely. Both the crepe and the filling will have better flavor and texture.

❧

In choosing cantaloupes, you can be reasonably sure they are ripe if the webbing stands out distinctly from the melon. They'll be full of vitamins and minerals, too.

❧

I settle the argument about whether or not to wash mushrooms this way: Wash them in cool water and dry them at once with paper towels. It is not necessary to peel them, just be sure they are clean.

[165]

One very good use of a food processor: Chop any leftover cooked vegetables, buttered and seasoned, and freeze them in plastic bags. Use them as a base for cream soups. It's a good idea to label them — I don't, and then I'm embarrassed when someone asks what kind of soup it is.

❧

Wash both lettuce and spinach in lukewarm and then cold water. Place the leaves in a plastic bag and seal it. Punch one tiny hole in the bag and refrigerate. The leaves will stay fresh and crisp longer.

❧

Aged meat with bones will make a superior stock for soups; but canned and dehydrated bouillon will serve the same purpose with fewer calories.

❧

If mayonnaise separates, as it does sometimes if too cold or too hot, beat it into a well-beaten egg yolk, a little at a time, until it thickens.

❧

When bacon is to be crumbled or finely diced, I place it in the freezer for about an hour and then dice it *before* sautéing. It looks much better that way.

❧

Wine, beer, and oil-and-vinegar salad dressing can all be used as marinades to tenderize meat. Soak meat in the marinade of your choice for several hours before cooking.

❧

When buying any fish, be sure the flesh is firm and resilient and has no pronounced odor. Frozen fish spoils quickly once it is thawed, so don't keep it around too long.

⚘

Cooked shellfish will freeze well, but do not reheat it too long or it will become mushy or leathery, as often happens with lump crabmeat.

⚘

To peel fresh tomatoes, dip them in boiling water for 30 seconds, then cool and refrigerate them. The skin will peel off easily. Refrigerated, they will keep for several days.

⚘

Acorn squash has excellent flavor and texture when baked whole, like a potato. To serve: split it; remove seeds, season and butter.

⚘

For bread makers: To test for "double in bulk," press your fingertips into the dough. If the dent stays, the dough has doubled in bulk.

⚘

For table decorations, use fresh vegetables such as bunches of radishes and carrots, or a glossy handsome eggplant. They make a nice change from flowers and also act as an appetite depressant.

⚘

Get in the habit of using a nonstick vegetable product (like Pam) to spray pans for roasting, broiling, and sautéing. No calories to count, and the pans clean easily. It's especially useful for molded salads and gelatin desserts — because they slide easily from the mold, their beauty is not destroyed by hot water dipping and knife digging.

❧

At one of my cooking schools, when I suggested using sliced hard-boiled eggs as a garnish, a young lady asked, "Do you peel the eggs before you slice them?" "No," I answered, "not if you like the shells."

❧

To allow your elegant smoked turkey to achieve perfection, place it in an open roaster in a slow oven, 250°F–300°F/ 120°C–150°C, for several hours. Baste every 20 minutes with melted margarine heated with white wine. Finish basting with the pan drippings and you will have a beautiful brown turkey, tender and mellow.

❧

Dieting isn't deadly at all when you can enjoy green turtle consommé sparked with crabmeat, or fresh red snapper with grapefruit, or roast squab in white wine as part of your diet regimen.

❧

Gazpacho is a good bad-temper medicine. I keep a gallon of it around at all times.

❧

I think it is much more flattering to ask your guests into the kitchen while you prepare dinner than to ask them to sit in the living room while you disappear.

❧

When planning a dinner, always prepare two desserts: one

high in calories and one low. I sometimes use a beautiful fruit centerpiece, and when the time comes I tell the guests the fruit is the dessert.

❦

Do less stirring. Don't pat and fuss with food. Be adventurous, but use a light hand with herbs and spices. A bit of soy, a dusting of spice — not a lot.

❦

A good theme for sensible eating is balance — nutritional and decorative — so that the dieter can lose weight, stay healthy, and enjoy eating.

❦

Think thin and you will automatically say "No, thank you" to the extra calories from bread and highly starchy foods.

❦

Meat loaf baked in an angel food cake pan seems to have a special flavor.

❦

While you're cutting back on calories, feed the eye by serving foods beautifully. For instance, a clear soup can be served in a shallow crystal bowl, with a green leaf from the garden inserted between the bowl and the plate.

❦

We all eat too much — it's Sunday dinner every day.

❦

It's the taste that counts.

[169]

Advice to dieters: Keep your mouth shut. You can prepare, serve, and eat low-calorie meals that are filling and attractive; if you don't go around talking about it, others will not know you are dieting. Forget the old idea that to diet you must suffer.

❦

Thinning a salad dressing with water leaves nothing but the flavor, and that's what you want anyway.

❦

Tomato juice is more fun to drink if you serve it in a stemmed, crystal wine glass with a cucumber stick in it.

❦

Never serve anything on toast except a sandwich.

❦

Fresh fruit tastes fresher in large pieces. Anything chopped tastes better and lasts longer than anything ground.

❦

Serve a whole artichoke rather than canned hearts. It takes a lot longer to eat it, so you may be tired of eating when you get through, and you probably won't want a great deal more that meal.

❦

Sharing good food — that's entertaining.

❦

Always pay attention to details. Coordinate place mats, napkins, the decorative greenery on the plates, the type of serving dishes, and the china you choose.

Food does not have to be expensive; it just has to be GOOD.

❦

When you aren't serving many calories, serve them on your best china and decorate the plate with fresh flowers, grape leaves, or croton leaves — anything you can't eat.

❦

It is a fact that a spoonful of puréed strawberries poured over any fruit lifts that fruit out of the ordinary. And when you serve large berries, there is nothing more refreshing to dip them into than the puréed fruit.

❦

Great standby low-calorie items to keep in the pantry are water-packed, canned artichoke hearts, celery hearts, mandarin oranges, and pineapple.

❦

The Jerusalem artichoke is a low-calorie bonanza. The small brown vegetable may be eaten raw and is crunchy and flavorful in salads or in any recipe calling for water chestnuts. When scraped, sliced, and steamed, it's often mistaken for potato.

❦

Chopped parsley is good on nearly all green vegetables.

❦

If you use a patchwork quilt for a tablecloth, the table will look filled before you begin. The trick is to make it look as if there is a lot to eat.

❦

You are never too young or too old to be a good cook.

Salsify, with a flavor somewhere between celery and parsnips, can be a delicious and surprisingly popular vegetable. It also comes canned and needs only seasoning with salt and pepper. You can add a dollop of cream if you are not dieting.

❧

Not new but still such a nice way to begin or end a meal: Grapefruit sectioned, sprinkled with a little cinnamon, and baked at 300°F/150°C for 10 minutes. Run it under the broiler to brown it, or leave it in the oven until the edges are brown. Before heating it you can sprinkle it with one tablespoon of tequila, which burns away but leaves a different and good taste.

❧

Don't be afraid to use your hands when cooking — and not just when you knead bread dough.

❧

Instead of heavy dressing, add a grating of cheese to salads; for meats, add a bit of soy sauce or a splash of wine instead of thick gravies; and try a dusting of spice sometimes on dessert, instead of a rich topping.

❧

Fruit centerpieces can be so pleasant: strawberries in a wicker basket, for instance, or pyramids of apples and grapes, or oranges and lemons. For an informal brunch build a pyramid of blueberry muffins that will be eaten up by the end of the meal.

❧

Why not serve a sundae that has the ice cream on top and the fruit on the bottom?

Why not serve escargots in edible pastry shells instead of the ever-so-slightly unappealing snail shells?

❧

Perk up a tossed green salad by adding small shrimp; or substitute a crystal bowlful of marinated vegetables like asparagus, cauliflower, celery, zucchini, and Brussels sprouts. Cucumber, green onions, and radishes may be added just before serving. It is colorful, refreshing, and good for you.

❧

A simple and attractive fresh fruit dessert is a compote of fresh peaches, steamed, skinned, and then cooked a few minutes in a sugar syrup.

❧

Don't save candles just for birthdays. Use long, slim Danish tapers on any handsome cake and celebrate any occasion.

❧

When you reach forty-five or fifty, reduce the salt in your diet. Use a grinding of fresh vegetables instead, or grated lemon peel. To be even smarter, begin at age 35 by *replacing* salt with other interesting seasonings.

❧

Always turn off the telephone when you are cooking something special that demands your full attention. More food has been ruined by the cook's answering the telephone than in any other way. *Never* answer the telephone when you are making jelly.

❧

There is an endless variety of food in our rich country. Often, however, Americans have a blind spot and see only green beans and lettuce, steaks and hamburgers. Enlarge your food horizons. Try everything you see in the produce department. Ask questions about new and unusual foods and introduce your family to them.

❧

You can add to the success of a meal by serving each dish in the right container. Don't go out and buy one — use something unexpected that you already have in your home. For example, a soup tureen filled with chopped ice is the perfect container for a glass bowl of fresh fruits cut in large pieces and covered with puréed frozen strawberries.

❧

Remember, when cooking with spirits, always use what you would drink — the better the spirits, the better the product.

❧

For new cooks there is one word of caution: Keep it simple.

❧

Use flank steak instead of more expensive cuts. Marinate it or not, then broil it and slice it thin. It's delicious. So many recipes recommend wrapping a flank steak around a bread dressing, and then all you have is a tough piece of meat.

❧

Yesterday has gone by; we can do nothing about it. Tomorrow is not yet here, and we can do something to make it more pleasant, especially gastronomically. Give freely of your own time and prepare delightful meals for your family. It is a loving way to spread health and happiness.

PART V

Glossary of Frequently Used Cooking Terms
Caloric Content of Common Food Items
Index

Glossary of Frequently Used Cooking Terms

Bake: to cook by dry heat in an oven.

Baste: to pour liquid over food — for example, meat — while cooking, to keep it moist.

Blanch: to immerse briefly in boiling water.

Boil: to cook in a liquid that has been heated to bubbling. "To boil 1 minute" means to start timing when the liquid begins to bubble.

Bone: to remove bones.

Broil: to cook under or over direct dry heat.

Chop: to cut in small pieces with a knife or chopper.

Correct seasonings: to adjust seasonings to your taste.

Cube: to cut in small squares with a knife.

Grate: to reduce food to shreds or powder by rubbing it against a grater or passing it through a mechanical device.

Julienne: to cut into matchstick pieces.

Mince: to cut in very small pieces with a knife or chopper.

Pan broil: to cook in a dry hot pan. You can spray the pan lightly with a vegetable preparation (such as Pam) to make cleaning the pan easier.

Poach: to cook in designated liquids that have been heated to just below boiling point.

Purée: to put through a sieve, blender, or food processor.

Roast: to cook uncovered in an oven by dry heat.

Sauté: to fry lightly in fat in a skillet.

Seed: to remove seeds.

Shred: to cut or tear in thin pieces, using a rasper, a mechanical shredder, or by hand.

Skewer: to fasten meat, vegetables, or fruit together on a long wooden, metal, or bamboo pin.

Sliver: to cut in thin pieces (I like them cut diagonally).

Snip: to cut in small pieces, diagonally, with scissors.

Steam: to cook over or surrounded by steam.

Stir-fry: to cook over high heat, using very little fat, and briskly tossing or stirring with a fork or spatula. This is an Oriental culinary method, especially good for low-calorie cooking. Best to use a wok, but a skillet is a fine substitute.

Caloric Content of Common Food Items and Beverages

	Approximate Calories
Apple, medium size with skin	80
Apple, medium size, peeled	64
Apple juice, canned, ½ cup	59
Applesauce, unsweetened, ½ cup	50
Artichoke, fresh, boiled	40
Artichoke hearts, frozen or water packed, 3 ounces (5)	20
Asparagus, fresh or frozen, 3 stalks	9
Avocado, ½ medium	185
Bacon, 1 thin slice cooked crisp and dry	30
Bamboo shoots, ½ pound	20
Banana, ½ small	41
Bean sprouts, ½ cup	19
Beef, lean, 3 ounces	215
Beef broth, 8 ounces	31
Beets, ½ cup	29
Blueberries, fresh, ½ cup	45
Bran cereal, pure, ½ cup	95
Bread, white, 1 slice	65
Bread, whole wheat, 1 slice	65
Broccoli, cooked, ½ cup	30

	Approximate Calories
Brussels sprouts, ½ cup	28
Butter, 1 tablespoon	102
Buttermilk, skim, 1 cup	88
Cabbage, ½ cup	11
Cabbage, Chinese, ½ cup	6
Canadian bacon, 1 ounce	52
Cantaloupe, ½ medium	60
Carrots, ½ cup	23
Casaba melon, ⅛	38
Catsup, 1 tablespoon	16
Cauliflower, ½ cup	15
Caviar, 1 ounce	75
Celery, ½ cup	10
Cheese, Cheddar, 1-inch cube	68
Cheese, Gruyère, 1 ounce	115
Cheese, Parmesan, grated, 1 tablespoon	23
Cheese, Roquefort, 1 ounce	111
Cheese, Swiss, 1 ounce	104
Cheez Whiz, 1 ounce	91
Cherries, fresh, ½ cup	41
Chicken, cooked, 1 ounce of meat, no skin	43
Chili sauce, 1 tablespoon	16
Chutney, 1 tablespoon	53
Clams, 4 or 5 medium	56
Clam juice, 1 cup	46
Clorets chewing gum, 1 piece	5
Cocoa, dry, 1 tablespoon	14
Cod, fresh, 4 ounces	89
Coffee, 1 cup	2
Coffee, decaffeinated, 1 cup	3
Cottage cheese, 4 ounces	100
Cream substitute (Coffee-Mate), 1 teaspoon	11
Corn chips, 1 ounce	164
Corn kernels, ½ cup	69
Corn on cob, 1 medium	74
Corned beef, 2 ounces	200

Cornstarch, 1 tablespoon	30
Crabmeat, Alaska, 4 ounces	116
Crabmeat, lump, ½ cup	50
Crackers, club, 1 piece	15
Crackers, graham, 1 piece	17
Crackers, saltines, 1 piece	12
Crackers, OTC, 1 piece	23
Crackers, oyster, ½ cup	60
Crackers, Ritz, 1 piece	15
Cranberries, ½ cup	22
Cranberry juice, ½ cup	82
Cream, half and half, 1 tablespoon	20
Cream, whipping, 1 tablespoon	45
Cream, sour, 1 tablespoon	29
Cream cheese, 1 ounce	106
Cucumber, ½ cup	8
Curry powder, 1 tablespoon	12
Egg, 1 medium	72
Egg white, 1 medium	15
Egg yolk, 1 medium	52
Eggplant, 1 medium	92
Enchilada, average, 1	185
English muffin	140
Farmer cheese, 1 tablespoon	19
Fat, vegetable, 1 tablespoon	111
Figs, fresh, 1 small	30
Flounder, 5 ounces	118
Flour, carob, 1 ounce	50
Flour, gluten, 1 ounce	108
Flour, soy bean, 1 ounce	101
Flour, wheat, 1 ounce	102
Flour, self-rising, 1 ounce	99
Frankfurter, 1	101
Garlic, 1 ounce	39
Gelatin, 1 tablespoon	23
Ginger root, skinned, 1 ounce	14

Grapes, ½ cup (10)	34
Grape juice, sweetened, ½ cup	104
Grape juice, unsweetened, 4 ounces	80
Grapefruit, ½	55
Grapefruit sections, 1 cup	80
Green beans, ½ cup	18
Halibut, 4 ounces	114
Ham, 2 ounces	106
Honey, 1 tablespoon	64
Honeydew melon, ⅛	50
Ice cream, rich, ½ cup	164
Ice milk, hardened, ½ cup	100
Jerusalem artichoke, ½ cup	25
Lamb, lean, cooked, 2 ounces	105
Leeks, sliced, 2 ounces	30
Lemon, 1 medium	20
Lemon juice, 1 tablespoon	4
Lettuce, soft, 1 head	23
Lettuce, iceberg, 8 ounces	30
Lettuce, iceberg, chopped, 1 cup	10
Lettuce, romaine, chopped, 1 cup	8
Lima beans, baby, 2 ounces	70
Lime, 1	19
Liver, calf, raw, 2 ounces	80
Liver, chicken, raw, 2 ounces	73
Lobster, 2 ounces	52
Macadamia nuts, 1 ounce	218
Macaroni, cooked, ½ cup	78
Mandarin oranges, canned, low calorie, ½ cup	31
Mango, ½ cup	56
Maple syrup, 1 tablespoon	50
Margarine, 1 tablespoon	102
Margarine, imitation, 1 tablespoon	50
Margarine, whipped, 1 tablespoon	68
Mayonnaise, 1 tablespoon	101
Milk, goat, 1 cup	163

Milk, skim, 1 cup	88
Milk, whole, 1 cup	160
Mushrooms, canned, sliced, ½ cup	17
Mushrooms, fresh, sliced, ½ cup	13
Nectarine, ½ cup	70
Oil, vegetable, 1 tablespoon	120
Okra, 8 medium	24
Olives, large, 1	10
Onion, ½ cup	22
Onions, green, 3 small	14
Orange, 1	71
Orange juice, ½ cup	41
Orange sections, ½ cup	42
Oysters, raw, 1 medium	7
Papaya, ½	60
Parsley, 1 tablespoon	1
Parsnip, ½ cup	51
Peas, cooked, ½ cup	57
Pea pods, ½ cup	50
Peach, fresh, 1 average size	38
Peanut butter, 1 tablespoon	94
Peanuts, dry roasted, 1 ounce	170
Peanuts, shelled, with skins, 1 ounce	172
Pear, fresh, 1	100
Pecans, shelled, halves, ½ cup	370
Pepper, green, 1 medium	16
Pepper, red, 1 medium	23
Persimmon, ½ cup	144
Pickles, dill, 1	3
Pie crust, 9-inch, 1	675
Pie crust, 1/6	112
Pimiento, ½ cup	31
Pineapple, ½ cup	40
Pistachio nuts, 1 tablespoon	46
Plum, damson, ½ cup	75
Pompano, 4 ounces	188

Popcorn, oil and salt, 1 cup	64
Popover, 1 average	112
Pork, roasted, 4 ounces	277
Pork sausage, 1 ounce	142
Potato, 1 medium	88
Potato chips, 10	113
Pound cake, 1 slice	150
Pretzels, 1 small	4
Prunes, cooked without sugar, 5 medium	119
Prune juice, ½ cup	88
Pumpkin, canned, ½ cup	40
Radish, 4 small	6
Raisins, 1 tablespoon	26
Raspberries, fresh, ½ cup	35
Raspberries, frozen, ½ cup	122
Rice, brown, ½ cup cooked	116
Rice, white, ½ cup cooked	111
Rice, wild, ½ cup cooked	288
Rutabaga, diced, ½ cup	30
Salmon, 2 ounces	104
Salmon, smoked, 1 ounce	50
Salsify, canned, ½ cup	79
Salt, any quantity	0
Sardines, in oil, 1 3¾-ounce can	167
Sauerkraut, ½ cup	21
Scallops, raw, ½ cup	92
Sesame seeds, 1 ounce	165
Shad, 4 ounces	228
Shallots, 1 ounce	14
Shrimp in shell, 1 pound	526
Shrimp, meat only, ½ cup	103
Sole, 4 ounces	90
Spinach, trimmed, raw, 1 cup	14
Squab, meat only, 4 ounces	161
Squash, acorn, ½ cup	56
Squash, yellow, ½ cup sliced	18

Squash, zucchini, ½ cup sliced thin	9
Sugar, brown, 1 tablespoon	49
Sugar, confectioners', 1 tablespoon	31
Sugar, granulated, 1 tablespoon	46
Sweetbreads, calf, 4 ounces	188
Sweet potato, 1 medium	152
Tangerine, 1 medium	40
Tea, 1 bag	1
Tomato, 1 medium	26
Tomato, canned, ½ cup	25
Tomato juice, ½ cup	23
Tongue, pickled, 1 ounce	76
Tortilla, 1	64
Trout, boned, 4 ounces	125
Tuna, water-packed, 1 6½-ounce can	240
Turkey, roasted, 2 ounces sliced	108
Turnip, diced, ½ cup	18
Turnip greens, cooked, ½ cup	14
Turtle meat, 2 ounces	60
Vanilla extract, 1 teaspoon	8
Veal chop, 4 ounces	245
Veal loin, roasted, 2 ounces	135
Vinegar, 1 tablespoon	2
Walnuts, ½ cup shelled	326
Water chestnuts, 2 ounces	36
Watercress, ½ cup	3
Watermelon, ½ cup	21
Wheat germ, 1 ounce	103
Whitefish, 4 ounces	177
Whitefish, smoked, 4 ounces	177
Yeast, compressed, 1 ounce	25
Yeast, dry, 1 tablespoon	23
Yogurt, skim, ½ cup	62
Beer, 12 ounces	150
Brandy, flavored, 1 ounce	75

	Approximate Calories
Champagne, 3 ounces	75
Distilled liquors, 80 proof, 1 ounce	65
Distilled liquors, 100 proof, 1 ounce	82
Wines, dessert, 3 ounces	120
Wines, dry red, 3 ounces	88
Wines, dry white, 3 ounces	75

Index

References to the menus appear in italic.

Acorn squash, 167
Alcohol, 12
Almond Soufflé, Cold Choco-
 late, 138
 Crab and, *34*, 74
Antipasto Salad, 27, 59
Apple Pie, Cheddar Cheese, 144
Apple Pudding, 136
Apple Sherbet, *34*, 122
Apples, Baked, 126
 Stewed, *42*, 128
 Wild Rice and, 160
Apricot Sauce, 144
Apricot Soufflé, Cold, 140
Apricot Whip, Hot, *38*, 131
Artichoke Soufflé, *28*, 89
Artichokes, 170, 171
Artichokes Stuffed with Crab-
 meat, *33*, 65
Asparagus Salad, 153

Bacon, crumbled, 166
Baked Apples, 126
Baked Custard, *22*, *28*, 125
Beans, Green
 Dilled, 81
 in Mustard Sauce, *42*, 62
 Mushrooms Stuffed with, *32*,
  88
 Polonaise, *33*, *43*, 82
Beef, Filet of, with Lobster
 Tail, *37*, 115
 Oriental, 27, 115
 Sautéed, with Leeks and
  Mushrooms, 161
Beet and Yogurt Soup, *24*, 54
Bisque, Oyster, *44*, 49
Borscht, Quick, 57
Bouillon, Potassium, 57
Bran Muffins, Refrigerator, 148

Bread making, testing for "double in bulk" in, 167
Breads and cereals, whole grain, 12
Breakfast, eggs for, 19
    fruits for, 18
    menu suggestions for, 17–19
Breast of Chicken, Fruited, *35*, 101
Breast of Chicken Dublin Style, *38*, 101
Breast of Chicken Piquante, *34*, 103
Buttermilk Dressing, *28*, *30*, *37*, 69
Buttermilk Sherbet, Strawberry, *34*, 122

Caloric content of common food items and beverages, 179–85
Cantaloupes, choosing, 165
Caramel Soufflé, 139
Carob Ice Cream, 123
Carrot Soup, *27*, 56
Carrots, Dilled, *30*, *38*, 81
Carrots in Vodka, *22*, 80
Carrots and Yellow Squash, *43*, 80
Celery, Gratin of, *24*, 81
Celery with Mustard Sauce, *37*, 62
Celery Root Salad, *26*, 64
Céléstine, Consommé, 53
Chantilly, Crabmeat, *24*, 96
Cheddar Cheese Apple Pie, 144
Cheese Custard, 75

Cheese Soufflé, Swiss, *36*, 73
Cheesecake, Low-Calorie, *24*, *35*, 124
Chicken, calories in, versus red meats, 11
    Ginger Roasted, *23*, 98
    Tandoori Roast, *25*, 99
Chicken, Breast of
    Dublin Style, *38*, 101
    Fruited, *35*, 101
    Piquante, *34*, 103
Chicken Breast in Foil, *43*, 104
Chicken in Champagne, *30*, 98
Chicken with Chanterelles, *44*, 100
Chicken Salad, Oriental, *40*, 106
Chicken Yakitori, *26*, 103
Chile Salad, Green, 152
Chile Torte, Green, *42*, 76
Chiles, green, 163
    Mary Wallbank's Pickled, 164
Chocolate Almond Soufflé, Cold, 138
Chocolate Cake, Netta Blanchard's Irish, 143
Chocolate Ice Cream, 123
Chocolate Mousse, Quick, 137
Chowder, Vegetable, *27*, 53
Clam and Mushroom Soup, *28*, 51
Cobb Salad, 151
Coffee Ice Cream, 123
Coffee Sponge, *39*, 130
Consommé, Jellied Vegetable, *21*, 54
Consommé Céléstine, *32*, 53

Coq au Vin, 22, 102
Cottage Cheese Dressing, 28, 72
Cottage Cheese Mousse, 39, 44, 78
Crab and Almond Soufflé, 34, 74
Crabmeat, Artichokes Stuffed with, 33, 65
Crabmeat Chantilly, 24, 96
Crabmeat and Grapefruit Salad, 28, 65
Cranberry Sherbet, 106, 119
Cream Cheese Soufflé, 156
Creamy Italian Dressing, 154
Crème Brulée, 135
Creole, Shrimp, 37, 95
Crepes, 165
    Souffléed, 141
Crisps, Gertie Cottle's, 165
Crown Roast of Lamb, 162
Crudité Salad, 32, 60
Cucumber stick, tomato juice with, 170
Cucumber Yogurt Soup, 35, 49
Curaçao, Hot Fruit, 145
Curried Yogurt Soup, 43, 47
Custard, Baked, 22, 125
    Cheese, 75
    English, 135
    Soft, 26, 124, 127

Dilled Carrots, 30, 38, 81
Dilled Green Beans, 81
Dinner and lunch menus (Monday through Saturday), 20–40
Dinner and supper or lunch menus (Sunday), 41–44
Dressings, salad, see Salad dressing(s)

Eggnog Ice Cream, 123
Eggplant and Mushroom Casserole, 157
Eggs, for breakfast, 19
    Spanish, 39, 77
    Teased, 155
Endive Salad, Mushroom and, 39, 61
Energy Equivalent Chart, 9–10
English Custard, 135
Escargots, 173

Fennel Salad, 153
Fettucine Alfredo, 155
Filet of Beef with Lobster Tail, 37, 115
Fish, buying, 166–67
Flank Steak, Marinated, 21, 116, 174
Florentine Tomatoes, 36, 88
Flounder, Stuffed, 36, 94
Frankfurters, Greenhouse, 161
French bread, spread for, 163
French Dressing, Sherry, 24, 27, 35, 36, 38, 44, 68
Frozen Orange Bowl, 33, 119
Fruit centerpieces, 172
Fruit Curaçao, Hot, 145
Fruit Ice Cream, 123
Fruited Breast of Chicken, 35, 101
Fruits for breakfast, 18

Garden Salad, 151
Gazpacho, 168
Gazpacho Blanco, 149
Gertie Cottle's Crisps, 165
Gin Soup, 150
Ginger Roasted Chicken, *23*, 98
Grand Marnier Sauce, 137
Grape Ice, *43*, 121
Grape Nut Ice Cream, 123
Grapefruit, baked, 172
Grapefruit Salad, Crabmeat and, *28*, 65
Gratin of Celery, *24*, 81
Green Beans, Dilled, 81
Mushrooms Stuffed with, *32*, 88
Green Beans in Mustard Sauce, *42*, 62
Green Beans Polonaise, *33*, *43*, 82
Green Chile Salad, 152
Green Chile Torte, *42*, 76
Green Chiles, 163
Mary Wallbank's Pickled, 164
Green Herb Dressing, *31*, *34*, *39*, *42*, 69
Green Salad Soup, *32*, 55
Greenhouse, The (Arlington, Texas), 3–7
Greenhouse Frankfurters, 161
Gumbo, Seafood, *43*, 50

Ice Cream, 172
Carob, 123
Chocolate, 123

Coffee, 123
Eggnog, 123
Fruit, 123
Grape Nut, 123
Mint, 123
Vanilla, *28*, *43*, 123
Ice(s), 118–19
Grape, *43*, 121
Orange, *24*, 120
Pineapple, with Peaches, 146
Irish Chocolate Cake, Netta Blanchard's, 143
Irish Tea Scones, 146
Italian Dressing, Creamy, 154

Jellied Vegetable Consommé, *21*, 54
Jerusalem Artichoke, 171
Jerusalem Artichoke Salad, Spinach and, with Creamy Italian Dressing, 154

Lamb, 164
Crown Roast of, 162
Lemon Roasted, *32*, 112
Lemon Roasted Lamb, *32*, 112
Lemon Snow Pudding Ring, *29*, 129
Lemon Soufflé, Cold, *42*, 126
Lemon Soup, Cold, *39*, 52
Lettuce, washing and storing, 166
Lobster Tail, Filet of Beef with, *37*, 115
Low-Calorie Cheesecake, *24*, *35*, 124

Lunch and dinner menus
(Monday through Saturday), 20–40
Lunch or supper and dinner
menus (Sunday), 41–44

Margarine, whipped, 11
Marinades, salad dressings used
as meat, 166
Marinated Flank Steak, *21*,
116, 174
Mary Wallbank's Pickled
Chiles, 164
Mayonnaise, 166
Meat loaf, baked in angel food
cake pan, 169
Menus
breakfast, 18–19
dinner and supper or lunch
(Sundays), 41–44
lunch and dinner (Monday
through Saturday), 20–40
Metric measurements, 13
Mimosa Dressing, *37*, 67
Mint Dressing, *28*, *29*, 71
Mint Ice Cream, 123
Minted Pea Soup, *26*, 55
Mousse, Cottage Cheese, *39*,
44, 78
Quick Chocolate, 137
Muffins, Orange, 147
Refrigerator Bran, 148
Mushroom Casserole, Eggplant
and, 157
Mushroom and Endive Salad,
39, 61

Mushroom Soup, Clam and, *28*,
51
Mushrooms, washing, 165
Mushrooms à la Grecque, 85
Mushrooms Stuffed with
Green Beans, *32*, 88
Mustard Sauce, Celery with,
37, 62
Green Beans with, *42*, 62

Netta Blanchard's Irish Choco-
late Cake, 143
Niçoise Dressing, *23*, 67
Niçoise Salad, *44*, 63
No Calorie Dressing, *32*, *40*,
70

Old-Fashioned Prune Whip,
43, 130
Onion Torte, *29*, 76
Onions and Peanuts, Scalloped,
158
Orange Bowl, Frozen, *33*, 119
Orange Ice, *24*, 120
Orange Muffins, 147
Orange Sauce, 125
Oranges, 164
Oriental Beef, 27, 115
Oriental Chicken Salad, *40*, 106
Osso Buco, *24*, 109
Oyster Bisque, *44*, 49

Papaya and Shrimp Salad, *37*,
66
Parfait, Wine Jelly, *42*, 127
Parsley, 171
Pea Soup, Minted, *26*, 55

Peaches, compote of fresh, 173
  Pineapple Ice with, 146
Pear Sherbet, *40*, 120
Pear Vinegar Dressing, 70
Pears Poached in Red Wine,
  23, 128
Peas in Sour Cream, 158
Pineapple Ice with Peaches, 146
Piquante, Salade, *39*, *63*
Poached Salmon, 91
Poached Turbot, *28*, 90
Polonaise, Green Beans, *33*, *43*,
  82
Potassium Bouillon, 57
Potato Salad, Watercress and,
  25, 67
Prune Whip, Old-Fashioned,
  43, 130
Pudding, Apple, 136
  Raspberry Sponge, *30*, 129
  Turnip, *21*, *34*, 86, 105
Pudding Ring, Lemon Snow,
  29, 129

Quiche, Shrimp and Spinach,
  25, 75
Quick Borscht, 57
Quick Chocolate Mousse, 137

Raspberry Sponge Pudding,
  30, 129
Ratatouille, *24*, *43*, 84
Red peppers, marinated, 164
Red Snapper with Grapefruit,
  34, 93
Red Wine Vinegar Dressing,
  21, 68

Refrigerator Bran Muffins, 148
Rice, Wild, and Apples, 160
Rice with Pine Nuts, 160
Roast Chicken, Tandoori, *25*,
  99
Roast of Lamb, Crown, 162
Roast Turkey in White Wine,
  105
Roast Veal with Herbs, 112
Roast Veal with Oranges, *40*,
  111
Roasted Lamb, Lemon, *32*, 112
Rock Cornish Hens Parmesan,
  28, 97
Roquefort Soup, Iced, *34*, 57

Salad Dressing(s)
  Buttermilk, *28*, *30*, *37*, 69
  Cottage Cheese, *28*, 72
  Creamy Italian, 154
  Green Herb, *31*, *34*, *39*, *42*,
    69
  Mimosa, *37*, 67
  Mint, *28*, *29*, 71
  Niçoise, *23*, 67
  No Calorie, *32*, *40*, 70
  Pear Vinegar, 70
  Red Wine Vinegar, *21*, 68
  Sesame, *26*, *44*, 71
  Sherry French, *24*, 27, *35*, *36*,
    38, *44*, 68
  thinning of, with water, 170
  used as meat marinades, 166
  Vinaigrette, 22, *23*, *24*, *25*,
    28, *29*, *33*, *38*, *44*, 67
  Yogurt, *32*, *34*, 72

Salad(s)
  Antipasto, 27, 59
  Artichokes Stuffed with
    Crabmeat, 65
  Asparagus, 153
  Celery with Mustard Sauce,
    62
  Celery Root, 26, 64
  Cobb, 151
  Crabmeat and Grapefruit,
    28, 65
  Crudité, 32, 60
  Fennel, 153
  Garden, 151
  Green Chile, 152
  Mushroom and Endive, 39,
    61
  Niçoise, 44, 63
  Oriental Chicken, 40, 106
  Papaya and Shrimp, 37, 66
  Piquante, 39, 63
  Spinach and Jerusalem Arti-
    choke, 154
  Watercress and Potato, 25,
    67
Salade Piquante, 39, 63
Salmon, Poached, 91
Salsify, 172
Salt substitutes, 11, 173
Sauce, Apricot, 141
  Grand Marnier, 137
  Mustard, 37, 62
  Orange, 22, 125
Sautéed Beef with Leeks and
    Mushrooms, 161
Scallion brushes, 93

Scalloped Onions and Peanuts,
    158
Scones, Irish Tea, 146
Seafood, calories in, versus red
    meats, 11
  frozen, 164
Seafood Gumbo, 43, 50
Sesame Dressing, 26, 44, 71
Shellfish, freezing cooked, 167
Sherbet(s), 118–19
  Apple, 34, 122
  Cranberry, 106, 119
  Pear, 40, 120
  Strawberry Buttermilk, 34,
    122
  Watermelon, 37, 121
Sherry French Dressing, 24, 27,
    35, 36, 38, 44, 68
Shrimp Creole, 37, 95
Shrimp Salad, Papaya and, 37,
    66
Shrimp and Spinach Quiche,
    25, 75
Soft Custard, 26, 43, 124, 127
Soft drinks, 12
Soufflé, Artichoke, 89
  Caramel, 139
  Cold Apricot, 140
  Cold Chocolate Almond, 138
  Cold Lemon, 42, 126
  Crab and Almond, 34, 74
  Cream Cheese, 156
  Swiss Cheese, 36, 73
Souffléed Crepes, 141
Soup, Beet and Yogurt, 24, 54
  Carrot, 27, 56
  Clam and Mushroom, 28, 51

Soup (*cont.*)
  Clear Tomato, *42*, 48
  Cold Lemon, *39*, 52
  Cucumber Yogurt, *35*, 49
  Curried Yogurt, *43*, 47
  Gin, 150
  Green Salad, *32*, 55
  Iced Roquefort, *34*, 57
  Minted Pea, *26*, 55
  stock for, 166
  Watercress, *40*, 52
Sour Cream, Peas in, 158
Spanish Eggs, *39*, 77
Spinach, Stir-fried, *21*, 83
  washing and storing, 166
Spinach and Jerusalem Arti-
    choke Salad with Creamy
    Italian Dressing, 154
Spinach Quiche, Shrimp and,
    25, 75
Sponge, Coffee, *39*, 130
Sponge Pudding, Raspberry,
    30, 129
Squab in White Wine, *43*, 107
Squash, acorn, 167
  Yellow, Carrots and, *43*, 80
Steak, Marinated Flank, 116,
    174
Stew, Veal, with Zucchini, *26*,
    113
Stewed Apples, *42*, 128
Stir-fried Spinach, *21*, 83
Stir-fried Vegetables, *23*, *37*, 86
Stock, soup, 166
Strawberries, puréed, poured
    over fruit, 171
Strawberries Excellent, 145

Strawberry Buttermilk Sherbet,
    34, 122
Stuffed Flounder, *36*, 94
Sugar substitutes, 11
Sweet 'N Low, 11
Swiss Cheese Soufflé, *36*, 73

Table decorations, use of fresh
    vegetables as, 167
Tandoori Roast Chicken, *25*,
    99
Tarragon Tomatoes, *33*, 87
Teased Eggs, 155
Tomato juice, cucumber stick
    with, 170
Tomato Soup, Clear, *42*, 47
Tomatoes, Florentine, *36*, 88
  peeling fresh, 167
  Tarragon, *33*, 87
Torte, Green Chile, *42*, 76
  Onion, *29*, 76
Trout with Red and Green
    Pepper Sauce, 92
Turbot, Poached, *28*, 90
Turkey, Roast, in White Wine,
    105, 168
Turnip Pudding, *21*, *34*, 86, 105

Vanilla Ice Cream, *28*, *43*, 123
Veal, Roast
  with Herbs, 112
  with Oranges, *40*, 111
Veal en Gelée, *42*, 114
Veal Loin Florentine, *33*, 110
Veal Piccata, 108
Veal Stew with Zucchini, *26*,
    113

Vege-Sal, 11
Vegetable Chowder, 27, 53
Vegetable Consommé, Jellied, 21, 54
Vegetable product, nonstick, for spraying pans, 167–68
Vegetables, fresh, used as table decorations, 167
  Stir-fried, 23, 37, 86
Vegetables à la Grecque, 27, 85
Vinaigrette Dressing, 22, 23, 24, 25, 28, 29, 33, 38, 44, 67
Vinegar Dressing, Pear, 70
  Red Wine, 68

Water, drinking, 10
Watercress and Potato Salad, 25, 67

Watercress Soup, 40, 52
Watermelon Sherbet, 37, 121
Whip, Hot Apricot, 38, 131
  Old-Fashioned Prune, 43, 130
Wild Rice and Apples, 160
Wine Jelly Parfait, 42, 127
Wines, 12

Yellow Squash, Carrots and, 43, 80
Yogurt Dressing, 32, 34, 72
Yogurt Soup, Beet and, 24, 54
  Cucumber, 35, 49
  Curried, 43, 47

Zucchini, 22, 35, 83
Zucchini Collage, 159
Zucchini Cups, 34, 82